Sit Down, God ... I'm Angry

R. F. Smith Jr.

To Jill —
with Fond
Memories —

Judson Press ® Valley Forge

Sit Down, God . . . I'm Angry

© 1997 Judson Press, Valley Forge, PA 19482-0851

Bible quotations in this volume are from the *Holy Bible,* King James Version, and from the Revised Standard Version of the Bible, copyright © 1946, 1952, 1971, by the Division of Christian Education of the National Council of Churches of Christ in the U.S.A. Used by permission.

Library of Congress Cataloging-in-Publication Data
Smith, R. F. (Robert Forest), 1931-
    Sit down, God— I'm angry / R.F. Smith, Jr.
    p. cm.
    ISBN 0-8170-1258-3 (pbk. : alk. paper)
    1. Bereavement—Religious aspects—Christianity. 2. Anger—Religious aspects—Christianity. 3. Grief—Religious aspects—Christianity. 4. Consolation. 5. Smith, Robert Forest, 1960-1978. 6. Children—Death—Religious aspects—Christianity. I. Title.
BV4905.2.S612 1997
248.8'66—dc21   97-30

Printed in the U.S.A.

05 04 03 02 01 00 99 98 97

10 9 8 7 6 5 4 3

This book is lovingly dedicated to
my wife, Faye,
and our daughters, Becky and Rachel,
for their courage in living the events in this book and
for their encouragement as I wrote about them.

Also to

Fifth Avenue Baptist Church,
my church family,
whose many touches helped with healing.

In memory of Robert Forest Smith III
(1960-1978)

Contents

Foreword

Somewhere in the workplace of creation the decision was made to equip humans with the capacity to experience emotions. This ability would bring them indescribable pleasure and unbearable pain. Emotions would also cloud their judgment, often resulting in erratic, illogical, and destructive behavior. As a counselor I have listened to numerous stories of how perfectly rational, intelligent, stable people lost everything because they succumbed to an emotion that distorted their pasts, destroyed their futures, and turned their presents into living nightmares. Conversely, others deny or sublimate their feelings, even to the point of destroying themselves physically, emotionally, and spiritually and negatively affecting their personal relationships.

The value of this book is that the author focuses on anger, an emotion that many of us find difficult to deal with in times of grief. Many psychologists believe that anger is the number-one killer emotion and is the anvil that makes or breaks relationships, yet people often try to deny its existence.

Dr. Smith goes further into "forbidden" territory by daring to express his anger at God. This correlation is especially troubling to those who were children in the 1950s or earlier. These generations were taught to be respectful, especially of elders, for failure to do so would bring swift and dire consequences. To rage at God, the ultimate authority who could punish in an instant, was unthinkable. But think it we did, without ever sharing those thoughts. Thus, guilt was birthed, giving anger a sibling to assist in our debilitation.

This book offers the assurance that anger is a normal emotion that is neither good nor bad within itself. The way it is expressed determines whether it will have positive or negative consequences.

I am convinced that expressing anger at God is not only normal but also necessary for authentic healing to take place. God both understands and accepts his children's outbursts when they are faced with crushing burdens. Never confronting God prolongs the night of suffering and delays the morning of peace.

The author's insistence that one cannot walk with unresolved anger forever, lest he or she die, is at the heart of the healing process. It must be left behind or one will forfeit the future. Walking *through the valley*, not dwelling there, is what the Smiths proclaim and practice. By word and deed they show us how to do it.

The power of this book is derived from the timing of the penned words. It is not a reconstruction from memory where time has softened the edges. Rather it is a transfer of notes from a journal, notes written in hospital waiting rooms and the bedroom of a young man who will not be returning to claim his belongings. The words of this book were written by one who has walked amid the white-hot lightning and deafening thunder.

For over thirty years I have been in a family-life practice, and this book is must reading for those who have experienced a deep hurt, especially if they perceive themselves as not deserving to be so wounded. It is a valuable gift from caring people to those who rage but find no peace. It is an essential resource for church libraries and pastors and should be handed to every church member who descends into the valley.

It was my privilege to be a guest in the Smith home and to be their friend for over twenty years. What you are about to read is true. No literary license was taken. Prepare to go on a journey that can change your life. To my friends, the Smiths, I offer the words of Tagore: "Death is not extinguishing the light. It is putting out the lamp because the dawn has come."

The dawn has come for their son, Forest. It will for each of us.

Dr. Charles V. Petty, President
Family Success Unlimited
Raleigh, N.C.

Preface

When I signed a contract for this book with Judson Press, the church graciously granted an extra three weeks to my annual study leave so that I could write it. Using vacation time, I calculated I could complete the book about our son Forest and our pilgrimage after his death that I had written in my mind over the past eighteen years.

In June, Faye and I made the three-hundred-mile trip to the foothills of North Carolina, loaded with computer, printer, boxes and boxes of books, as well as memorabilia of our deceased son. We arrived at the home of my childhood and youth, The Ophelia-Forest (named for my mother, Ophelia Benfield Smith, and my father, Robert Forest Smith Sr.), where we unloaded our overstuffed car. That evening we called friends of years past and scheduled a dinner for the next evening in nearby Blowing Rock, a lovely mountain resort. As I prepared to write the book, I needed to change gears from a hectic week in the parish. We figured an evening in our beloved mountains with these friends would ease the transition.

We met Barbara and Roscoe McNeil, whose friendship spanned some thirty-five years, at a mall prior to dinner. While our wives shopped, Roscoe and I sat on a bench in the cool of the evening, talking.

Then Roscoe leveled a question that I had not anticipated: "Why are you writing this book about Forest?" Before I could answer, he said, "It's been nearly eighteen years. We watched you go through it. It was terrible. Why are you opening all this up again?"

I'm not sure how I answered Roscoe. We always said to each other whatever was on our minds, but frankly, his blunt question rattled me. If the truth be admitted, maybe I resented his probing question.

The next morning in my study, which had been my bedroom during my turbulent teenage years, I started reading the early pages of the journal I had kept since Forest's death. Turbulence again. Sobs racked my body, and tears flowed as they had eighteen years ago.

Roscoe's question started making sense. "Why *am* I writing this book?" For most of the summer I asked that question over and over. The hardest thing I've ever experienced was Forest's death. The second hardest was writing the pages that follow. I would read my aging journal for an hour and cry for an hour. I'd write for an hour and cry for an hour as I read what I had written.

After only three days of writing, I slammed shut my study door, went downstairs, and told Faye, "If I were not under contract, I'd quit! Right now. I'd not read another journal page or write another word. I don't think I can do this." I flopped my weakening body on the couch, pulled a pillow over my head, and cried as Faye, ever my comforter, soothed my pain with words and touch.

The first chapters were the most painful. As time elapsed and the stack of completed pages grew higher, I discovered the pain was less. I still cried at some points, but my sobs were softer.

But the question kept coming back: "Why are you writing this book?"

There are several reasons, but chiefly three.

First, soon after Forest died, I promised I would write a book about him. I'm not sure whom I promised. Myself, mostly, I guess. And the family. And Forest's friends. Perhaps Forest. But the book was something I had wanted to write since his death. All sons are special, and every parent properly feels that. I wanted people to know this young man who was unique in so many ways. I wanted people to know Forest and be blessed by his brief but dynamic life.

Second, my pilgrimage following his death was severe in many respects. I had read many books about grief, and each dealt with anger as part of the process. But the anger I felt was far more intense and devastating than I had read about and anticipated.

I wanted to say to people losing loved ones, especially parents losing children, that anger is real, that it is okay to admit it and definitely appropriate to express anger to God. He can take it. (After all, God *does know* we are mad!)

Third, I wanted to say to parents losing children, *There is life for you after their death.* At first, you're not sure you will ever live again. You are certain you will never laugh again. But you will. You will always walk with a limp, but you will walk again.

In this book I hope the reader will discover not only the basic steps in processing personal grief but ways and means of ministering to friends who lose loved ones. In our family's journey through the valley of death, we found some handles to hold onto as we made our way. And we also discovered some things *not* to do or say when friends are struggling through the wilderness of grief. Helping others in their time of sorrow is measured as much by what we don't say as by what we do say. I think the reader will find certain ways to lighten a friend's load rather than add to the burden.

I have simply told my story and the story of our family as we journeyed along after the tragic loss of a son and brother. It is my hope that the reader will travel with me over this treacherous terrain and perhaps receive insight and comfort even in the "valley of the shadow."

The Ophelia-Forest
Summer 1996

Acknowledgments

Writers may write alone, but no one publishes alone. Among the many persons who helped with this book, I especially appreciate the patience, challenge, and expertise that came from the members of the Judson Press staff: Kristy Arnesen Pullen, Mary M. Nicol, and Victoria W. McGoey; and my staff, in particular Donna Akers, who constantly typed, retyped, mailed drafts, and performed the dozens of tasks necessary for making this book possible.

Introduction

"God, get in your Black Chair. I've got some things I need to say," I yelled, as I fell to my knees in a hospital waiting room, surrounded by family, physicians, and friends.

We had just lost Forest, our seventeen-year-old son. Our only son. He had been injured in a water-skiing accident eight days before. Waving to girls on the shore, he did not see the fishing pier jutting into the lake. He hit it full speed. For over a week he lay in a coma, mortally wounded by sixty-some bruises on his brain. At 1:05 A.M., September 12, 1978, he died. And I was mad. I didn't ask, I ordered God to get in his Black Chair.

Only my wife and children knew what I meant. The Black Chair incident happened when our children were twelve, ten, and eight. My wife, Faye, and I were in our bedroom reading the newspaper. She was relaxing on the bed, and I was sitting in my favorite black chair. Becky, Forest, and Rachel came in and stood in a stair-step line, military-like. Faye and I looked up from our papers.

Becky, the oldest, was spokesperson. "Dad, who do we tell off when we get mad?"

"What do you mean?" I asked.

"Well, when you and Mom get mad, you tell us off. So, who do we tell off when we get mad?"

"Me . . . your mother . . . both of us," I said.

They wagged their heads dramatically in the negative.

"No way," Becky said, and the other two nodded agreement.

"We don't dare tell you two off when we get mad. You'd get us!"

I saw their point. "Okay," I said. "Anytime I'm sitting in this black chair, you can tell me off. You can say anything you have on your mind." Their mother nodded agreement to the contract.

"Oh, no," they said, almost in unison. "You'd get mad and punish us."

I understood. The ground was not level. "Tell you what I'll do," I said, buying time and fumbling for a solution. "I can't promise I will not get mad, but I do promise I won't hold anything you say against you. I will not punish you for what you say."

The three children looked at each other, considering the contract, and then nodded agreement. "Okay," Becky said. "When can we get started?"

"Now," I said, but I was not braced for the ventilation of their anger. For the next thirty minutes they told me everything wrong and negative I had ever done and how they felt about it. The whole experience was a catharsis for them and a lesson for me.

In time, any chair where I was sitting became the Black Chair. All they had to say was, "Dad, are you in your Black Chair?" When I said yes, they were off and running. Sometimes I had to wear an emotional seatbelt because they'd really let me have it.

The Black Chair Philosophy, as it came to be called in our family, was perhaps the most creative and dynamic component in our parenting experience. The children would come to me or to their mother, ask for Black Chair time, and unload teenage frustrations and experimentations with no fear of reprisal. Anger was diffused, hurts healed, and wrongs righted as the Black Chair became part of our family experience.

So when Forest died, I was mad at God. Here was a young man who was everything a father would have ordered if given the privilege. He was all boy, deeply Christian, and committed to a career that would have blessed humanity and honored God.

But God let him die!

And, like my children who often were mad at me and put me in my Black Chair, I was mad at God and did the same. On that cold hospital floor I knelt, and for the next ten minutes I told God what I thought of him in no uncertain terms. I told him how senseless this death was, how wasted this life. I questioned his love in letting this happen. I doubted his power to do anything about it. I raved and ranted at the Most High God. When I finished I wiped the tears, and with them some of the burden was blotted away.

As I walked into the darkness that night, surrounded by understanding friends, I almost apologized for my audacity in taking on God so angrily. But I was stopped short by a psychiatrist, a close friend of the family who had been in the room during my tirade against God. "You have good precedent for expressing anger over the death of your son," he said, putting a comforting hand on my shoulder. "That's exactly what God did. When his son died, God quaked the earth and blackened the heavens. Don't you think God was mad?"

Although I had thought little about God's anger over the death of his son, I soon came to think intensely about my anger at God over the death of my son. Such anger is too often denied, especially if the death is untimely, premature, or the result of a tragic accident. And when anger is recognized by persons losing loved ones, it sometimes scares them.

The words of a young physician friend who was with us that night sum up the feelings of many people when anger against God surfaces. "You scared me to death with your anger at God," he said, half teasing, half not. "I thought sure he'd strike you dead and the rest of us would get scorched!"

In the Black Chair night with God I dumped out all I felt before my Creator, knowing I did not need to protect him; knowing that whatever I could dish out God could take. He took it and in time cooked it so I could digest it and get on with my life.

But his *cooking* and my *digesting* didn't happen with one Black Chair session. Just as my children needed many Black Chair episodes in their growth toward maturity, so I needed many Black Chair times with God as I made my journey through the "valley of the shadow."

The children learned from their first Black Chair set-to that they could ventilate anger and frustration without suffering negative consequences. And I learned that God could be trusted to handle my questions of doubt, my frustrated tirades bordering on blasphemy, and my struggles with anger that would ultimately enrich my faith without diminishing my commitment to God.

Just how God would use that Black Chair night to begin my healing is captured perhaps in the words of that same young physician, who wrote nearly ten years later on the thirty-fifth anniversary of my ordination:

> Perhaps the most spiritually exemplary evening in my life came during the most tragic of yours. In a tiny room just off neurointensive care at Baptist Hospital on the evening of Forest's death, I was witness to an example of Christian faith unsurpassed in my lifetime and one I will most surely never forget.
>
> You placed God in his "black chair" and ventilated your feelings to him in the most forthright way, but all the while your commitment remained steadfast and strong. Even then you were unknowingly ministering to one of your flock as I witnessed your faith at work.

My "faith at work," as the young doctor phrased it, demanded a lot of work in the weeks and months that followed. The work began almost immediately as I recalled a verse of Scripture that kept haunting me during the two-hour drive home from the hospital the night Forest died. The prophet Ezekiel had said: "At evening my wife died. And on the next morning I did as I was commanded" (Ezekiel 24:18 RSV). How could he do this? How could a man lose his wife in the evening and go about his daily run of duty the next morning? How could I *ever* go on, let alone the next day or even the next year?

This was my only son. He had my name and was proud of it, always putting the number *III* at the end when he signed anything. There was no door we could not go through together. We had plans. The night before, he had almost completed his application to my university alma mater, and he planned to enter, in time, its law school.

Parents are not supposed to bury their children; their children bury them. That's God's calendar; that's the way this whole plan for parents and children was put together. The question would not go away. Anger at God kept surfacing. And I cried.

During the next few weeks Ezekiel's verse rolled around and around in my mind and soul. Early one morning I came to the conclusion that something was missing in the prophet's account of his experience. He said his wife died in the *evening* and the next *morning* he did his duty. But he did not say what he did that *night!*

Though the prophet is silent about his experience during that
period, this stretch of time is most crucial for one who is dealing
with the experience of death. It is the bridge from what was and can
never be again to what is possible in the future.

One can only speculate about what happened with the prophet
during the long night of the soul; however, one can be sure there
was a night, whether recorded in a journal or not.

The *evening of death*, the *night of grief*, and the *morning of duty*
are three separate periods in the experience of losing loved ones;
yet it is difficult to draw lines separating them, especially the latter
two, because they keep bleeding into each other during the early
weeks and months after a loved one dies.

The *evening of death* brings its own shadows, casting long
ribbons of darkness and numbing every fiber of life. That darkness
etched my soul in ways I never dreamed possible.

PART 1

The Evening of Death

"At evening my wife died...." (Ezekiel 24:18)

Chapter One

Ezekiel said his wife died in the evening. We don't know how his wife died. An accident? A serious illness? Old age? We don't know, but we do know it was evening. He tells us that. She could have died anytime during the day, but when she died, it was evening for Ezekiel.

It is always evening when death comes to our loved ones. Always. The sun is setting. All nature knows this and prepares for night as evening shadows lengthen—animals instinctively gear down; flowers steel themselves against the impending darkness. Evening does come, and death does happen. Whatever can die does die—sometime, somewhere. And it is always evening.

Unlike nature, human nature is not so prepared. We plan for life, not death. And that is good, certainly. We should plan to live forever. That's what faith is all about—living forever. But there's an interruption in the forever-ness of life. We call it death. Most of us believe we can deal with our own death, but we're not so sure we can deal with the death of a loved one, especially if that loved one is a child.

My evening came on September 3, 1978, the Sunday of Labor Day weekend. Forest was water skiing with friends. Earlier in the afternoon he had phoned, wondering if he could spend a little more time on Lake Hickory near our home in North Carolina. We had planned to hit a few golf balls late in the afternoon and then barbecue some ribs, which we both loved. I told him to enjoy himself but really felt a bit disappointed about our golf plans. "I'll be home for dinner," he promised, "so have the grill going."

But time for dinner came, and Faye and I, along with Rachel, who had been skiing with them but had returned early, settled for a

cold sandwich on a hot evening. I wondered aloud whether Forest
would get home in time to finish his application for early admission
to Wake Forest University, which he had dreamed of attending all
his young life, and where Faye and I had met. On Saturday he had
roughed out the university's required essay about his life and his
hopes and dreams, but it needed polishing, he had told me.

"Oh, Dad," Rachel said. "You know he'll get it finished. Don't
worry about it," she chided, as she dashed out for some rendezvous
of sixteen-year-olds that only teenagers can conjure up on a lazy
Sunday evening.

Faye reminded me, "He wants to go to Wake Forest more than
anything in life. He'll get it finished. He's got tonight and much of
tomorrow." I mumbled something about Forest's putting things off
until the last minute at times and then smiled to myself, knowing
that with the biggies in his life he had always come through.

But Forest's essay for Wake Forest would never feel the careful
polishing of the budding young writer's touch. As I was finishing
my sandwich, the phone rang. "For you," Faye said. I took the call
in our bedroom, away from the television so she could watch *60
Minutes.*

"Are you Dr. Smith?" a soft female voice asked.

"Yes."

"Are you Dr. R. F. Smith Jr.?"

"Yes. Yes, I am."

"Dr. Smith, this is the emergency room at Glenn R. Frye Hospital. Your son Forest has been in an accident."

She said something else, but I can't remember what. A chilly
wave of something rushed over me like a hurricane out of control.
I sat down hard on the bed, twisting the telephone cord, trying to
focus. I was afraid of the next question I knew I had to ask, wanted
to ask, but I couldn't form the words. I don't know how long I sat
there, body shivering, reacting to the first freezing blow of the
young nurse's statement.

In those split seconds that seemed like an eternity in slow motion,
I computed that her voice was calm, not desperate or hopeless. But
I also knew that she was a professional, trained and experienced in

giving out bad news to shocked people. So I discounted her calmness and finally mustered courage to ask, "Is . . . he hurt . . . bad?"

I knew she had several options–*yes, no, we're not sure*, or, worst of all, *he has expired*. "He's unconscious right now, but we are working with him. It was a boating accident," she volunteered.

"We'll be there in a few minutes," I'm sure I said.

Turning from the phone, heading to tell Faye, one phrase kept banging in my head and gut: "No, God, no. Not my son, not my only son. Please, God, not him; not like this." My lips were moving, but no sound was coming out.

How do I tell his mother? What do I say to her? The relationship between them is so strong, so special, she might just pass out on me. Do I go by myself, survey the situation, talk with the doctors, and then come back and tell her?

The first impulse when tragedy strikes is to protect the family. That's commendable but counterproductive, especially over the long term. I have watched family members try with love and sensitivity to insulate other members of the family from the harsh blows of bad news. But such efforts often cause greater pain, like cutting off a cat's tail an inch at a time. Honesty is called for in such situations. I have often been chastised for giving too little information, but never for giving too much. And, too, when we try to protect loved ones from reality, we usually end up undermining trust. And trust is the one component so important when a family is facing the death of a loved one.

No, I reasoned, *we are a family, a team. We walk through valleys as well as on the mountains–together. And we'll face this together. Her special love for him, expressed in so many different ways, is strong, and she is a strong woman. She'll handle it, maybe better in the long run than you will,* I told myself.

"Faye," I said, as calmly as my shortened, not-so-calm breathing would allow. "Brother's been hurt. I think we ought to go to the hospital and check on him."

"Oh, my God," she blurted, more in prayer than in oath. "Where? When? How?" Her questions came with machine-gun speed.

"The lake. Boating. Skiing. Something. I'm not sure." My sentences were getting shorter, as my mind flirted with the dark edges of the worst that could happen to a guy who is everything parents could ask for in a son. "Let's go," I urged, as I started for the door. But she couldn't move. Her body froze, while newly formed crevices in her face deepened to receive the trickle of tears. I turned, took her in my arms, and for a few scared moments held her close as our hearts pounded together in a strange rhythm, a beat we'd never felt before.

I've learned that when bad news comes, we must be attentive to the immediate needs of those still standing on the battlefield of the negative experience. The short time between the nurse's first words and my internal discussion of how to tell my wife had given me an advantage she didn't have. I had to allow her time to catch up.

In ministering to families, I have at times watched family members rush beyond others who were still frozen or staggering from the bad news. Often they are impatient, wanting to get on with the process, rather insensitive to the struggles of the fellow wounded. Such actions stimulate anger and hostility, the last thing a family unit needs at that point. Time for embracing and supporting must be allowed before people can move ahead to what must be done.

"Tweety," I said, using the pet name we called each other in special and tender times. "I don't know what's going on, but whatever it is, we will face it together."

She nodded agreement, broke the embrace, reached for a tissue, and said, "I'm ready, Tweety, I'm ready."

We jumped in the first car in the driveway and, with lights flashing, made our way to the hospital. In a few minutes we were there, running toward the emergency room, past the scary-looking rescue squad vehicle and the uniformed attendants who seemed to know us and quickly opened the door.

"I'm R. F. Smith," I said, gasping for breath.

"Right this way, Dr. Smith," the receptionist said, not smiling. God, how I had hoped for a smile, for anything that would have said, "He's going to be okay."

We went through the forbidding doors with No ADMITTANCE stenciled on them in big, black letters. The room was alive with nurses. Doctors were moving about with charts and X-ray negatives, dressed in comfortable, casual shirts and trousers, having been summoned to the room of emergencies from tennis courts, golf courses, and family dinners.

The whole scene was so familiar. I had spent many hours in emergency rooms during the past twenty-five years, comforting and supporting church members. But this time it was different. I was not the pastor taking the arms of bewildered and hurting parents, guiding them to out-of-the way seats, getting them coffee, holding their hands, finding tissues for flooding eyes. This time I was in their seat, just as bewildered and hurting and confused as ever I had seen my parishioners.

We stood there for a few moments. Then a nurse—an old friend and a church member—came up, took our hands, and said, "The doctor will talk with you in a moment. Can I get you something?"

We shook our heads. "How is he?" I asked.

"He's still unconscious, but his vital signs are good," she said.

"Which room?" I wondered aloud.

"The back one," she pointed.

"Can I see him?"

"Surely, in just a moment. They're taking some X-rays just now."

About that time a young man, not more than twenty-nine or thirty, came up to us. "I'm Dr. Pitts. Your son is unconscious, but his vital signs are all good and steady. Our preliminary examination indicates he may be suffering a concussion." He told us that everything looked steady and sturdy, but he wanted to transfer Forest to a medical center for further neurological tests and evaluation.

"Baptist in Winston-Salem," I told him.

"Good," he said. "I'm a neurological resident there rotating through the hospital here. I'll call immediately and have them standing by when he gets there. I have one or two more tests to run before we put him in the ambulance. We'll have a respiratory therapist riding with him."

"Doctor, how bad is our son?" I asked.

His eyes dropped from ours; his fingers fiddled with the chart in his hands. "I'm really not sure, sir. He's a sick young man, but he's strong. His brain has suffered severe trauma."

"I understand, Doctor. Thank you. We'll follow the ambulance to Winston."

"I wish I could tell you more," he said, and his eyes supported his words.

As much as I wanted to, I didn't push him for answers. Doctors are human, limited in their ability to work magic or have all the answers. Maybe the reason I didn't push him was because I was afraid of his answers. I knew one thing: Forest was hurt badly, and the days ahead would be the hardest we had ever experienced.

The nurses did everything to make us comfortable. They took us to an empty examining room, and a young policeman who knew us brought coffee, asking if he could contact anyone for us.

"Rachel!" I suddenly remembered. "We've got to get in touch with her." I knew she was going by the home of our friends the Robertses on an errand before joining her friends for the evening. I called Earl and told him of the accident. Rachel had just left their home, but he would locate her.

A short while later I heard Rachel down the hall ask, "Is my father, Dr. Smith, here?" The nurse brought her through the swinging doors, and I moved to her.

"What's wrong, Dad? Why are you here?"

"It's Brother, honey, he's . . ." but I didn't finish. Her body stiffened in shock, and tears started. I put both arms around her and pulled her close, holding her tight as I often did during her sixteen years when some childhood hurt was more than she could take.

"Was it the boat?" she asked.

I nodded.

"How bad?"

"He's unconscious just now, but they are working with him. We hope he'll come around in a little while."

Pushing back from my embrace, she said, "I want to see him."

"In just a minute," I assured her.

"Right now, Dad. Now!" she demanded.

The nurse nodded approval, and we moved to the little curtained-off room with doctors and nurses and attendants crowded around him. They moved back so we could see him. He seemed asleep, just as I had seen him hundreds of times during his nearly eighteen years. The sleep this time was a bit more fretful, and he thrashed around more. He was moving all his limbs, which gave me some comfort, indicating he had not suffered paralysis.

Rachel stood there with me for a few minutes until her silent tears changed to sobs. She turned quickly and left the room. I caught up with her, slipped my arm around her, and walked back to the private room with her.

"Where did Mr. Roberts finally find you?" I asked.

"Who?"

"Earl Roberts. I asked him to find you."

"Dad, I haven't seen anyone," she said, stunned.

"Then . . . how did you get here?"

"I met you coming through town with your lights on. Forest had given me his billfold to keep for him when I left the lake. I was going back home to leave it because I knew he would need it tonight. When I saw you in the car I had this funny feeling something was wrong. Dad, you won't believe this, but I had this vision of a boating accident flash in my mind and I could see Forest in it. Then I turned around and fought heavy traffic to the hospital. Somehow I knew you would be here."

"Rachel," I said, still a bit confused. "There are three hospitals here. The bigger hospital is the one we usually use. How did you know to come here?"

"I don't know. It was just a feeling. Somehow I just knew you were here and something bad had happened." Then she added, "Dad, as you say, 'The two of us have the same brain, maybe just one brain split between us,'" and she forced a faint smile, the only smile our family would have for weeks to come.

The three of us sat together in our private room trying to sip coffee, attempting to work through the jumbled threads that were tying our souls in knots. We were scared, but we dared not tell each other. We didn't have to; our eyes betrayed us. Each was praying, and occasionally the moving lips emitted whispered tones. I remember only sketches of the whispered sounds and prayers in that little nightmarish room—"God, why?" "Father, what's going to happen?" "Dear God, please . . ." "My son . . . my little buddy." "O God, God." "My brother, my brother!"

Gradually we began to put the pieces of the accident together with the help of Forest's friend who had been pulling him with his boat, and other eyewitnesses. He was skiing in a cove. The water was calm, looking more like a giant mirror than a lake. Forest said it was time to go, but he wanted to make one more pass around the cove before he headed for the shore and home. Some people on a pier waved at him. He looked at them, but by the time he looked back he was too close to a pier to avoid hitting it. He made one desperate attempt to miss it, but his right leg and head hit it. Forest's friend and some bystanders pulled him from the water where he was lying face down. When they placed him on the pier, he tried to get up. He groaned and tried to say something. Oddly enough, there were no bruises on his head. They thought he was just knocked out and would soon come around. The rescue squad was called, and they raced him to the hospital.

I felt so sorry for Forest's young friend who had driven the boat. He stood in one corner of the waiting room. I went to him and told him we did not blame him in any way. He just stood there shaking his head. "I didn't take care of him, Dr. Smith, I didn't take care of him," he jerked the words out with deep emotion.

"But you did," I said. "You got him out of the water. You saved his life. Forest would have drowned. He's alive in there right now because you *did* take care of him. Look," I told him, "you gave Forest what he needed—friendship and fun. I don't have a boat, but you do. He loves skiing. He told me only last night that water skiing is the most relaxing sport he's ever done. He appreciated the time you gave him and the privilege of using your boat and skis. If there's any blame, it's on my shoulders—I taught him to ski! But I can't blame myself for teaching him to ski any more than you can blame yourself for pulling him with your boat. Now, look," I told the shaken young man, "when Forest comes out of this, he'll be right back out there, and he'll want you to pull him—and you will!"

Almost immediately when tragedy strikes, most of us seek to fix blame. That's normal. We wonder how such a calamity could have happened. What did we do? What did we *not* do? Certainly in many situations the blame can be leveled at someone. But I think it is important to withhold blame fixing until we are through the initial stages of the grief process, and evidence can be placed on the table of rational thinking.

People—especially friends and family members—involved in an accident in which someone is injured fix the blame immediately upon themselves whether justified or not. The last thing they need is to feel that we are holding them responsible. Maybe they are, but the hours immediately following the incident are not the time to judge.

I was tempted to blame myself by moving into the Land of If—*if* I had not taught Forest to ski, *if* I had insisted he come home early for our golf outing, if . . . if . . . if. The Land of If devastates. It's a merry-go-round island that goes faster and faster until dizziness comes, upsetting balance, creating chaos. It's a land where life stagnates, suffocates, and ultimately is destroyed. I spent some time in that land. Practically every grieving and hurting person sees that little island and washes up on its shores almost automatically. Pitching an overnight tent there is understandable and perhaps inevitable. But setting up a permanent residence is dangerous and can compound the tragedy that's being dealt with.

Faye and I were silent in the little Land of If as we drove home to pack our bags. We knew Forest was in good hands on the way to the North Carolina Baptist Hospital and Wake Forest's Bowman Gray School of Medicine, The Medical Center, some seventy miles away in Winston-Salem.

We hurriedly packed our bags and made a few phone calls. Becky was not at her apartment in Chapel Hill, where she lived since enrolling at the University of North Carolina. I decided I'd call her later that evening. I was on one phone and Faye on the other as we made calls to let friends know the situation. We had to let people know; we had to get our support system alerted and our prayer partners working.

I have learned that we can get sick by ourselves, but we cannot get well by ourselves. Healing is in the body—the community—of faith. Romans 15:1 (KJV) reminds us that "we then that are strong ought to bear the infirmities of the weak." In times past Faye and I were the strong, but now we were the weak. We needed help. And we reached out, letting people know the crisis and our pain.

The old adage "Laugh and the world laughs with you, weep and you weep alone" is true only if we make it so. We don't have to weep alone. Sow a friendship, and reap a harvest of support in times of crises. The world may not weep with you—that's not necessary—but enough people will gather around you *if* you have cultivated friendship and *if* you let them know. They cannot know from silence.

We pastors often complain that some of our members become sick, go the doctor, are admitted to the hospital, and never let us know. One member said to me after I finally discovered he was in the hospital, "Well, I just wondered how long it would take you to find out I was here!" I tried to be kind but did remind him that my seminary did not offer Detective Training 101.

Over the years I have encouraged people to create and maintain networks of support. Faye and I have kept a list of persons to be called in case of emergency. These friends are our first line of support, people we need around us. We never know what lies around the next curve, and the list of people on whom we can lean during crises is perhaps the most important list we can have. Just talking briefly with these supportive people gave us the energy we needed and would need desperately in the days ahead.

Just before we left, I went downstairs to my study and passed Forest's room. I slipped into his room, and sobs racked my body. I knelt by his unmade bed, twisted and chaotic from his hurried departure, and prayed. I don't remember what I said, something about asking God to take care of my son. I knelt in the same spot where I had knelt hundreds of times when he and I read the Bible and prayed together. I looked at his well-worn and much-read Bible.

Many times Forest invited me to "tuck him in," which actually meant, "read the Bible and pray." He never failed to read his Bible, no matter how late the hour. And when he was so tired, maybe too tired to read, he'd ask me to read to him. I used to tease him that he was the only guy I knew who had his own private chaplain. There was an openness about him that allowed me to walk on the sacred shores of his soul.

No incident was ever too small for him to ask God's help. Sometimes I wondered if he took too much of God's time about small incidents in his life. I kidded him about it one night. I shall never forget the seriousness of his clear blue eyes, and I knew I had teased at the wrong time about the wrong thing. But he didn't make me feel bad or guilty. He just said, "Dad, right now I need all the help I can get." The statement was sincere, and I hugged him tightly, thankful for a son whose trusting faith had much to teach me.

I did learn many things from him. He had a patience I envied. He granted that patience to people in endless quantities. I often stood amazed at how tolerant and understanding he was with all people. He seemed to give every person the benefit of the doubt. (That was his mother's genes working!) Frankly, sometimes I thought he was too understanding, too generous with his patience, but I was wrong. I saw how deeply people who experienced his patience loved him, respected him, and followed him. How a seventeen-year-old got so much of life together in such a short time, I'll never know. But he did, O God, how much he did. Forest made loving people look so easy. I often wondered where he got all that love. And he made faith in God look so simple, yet so profound. He seemed to operate on a different wavelength from the rest of us.

I used to watch him beat his beloved drums. Man, how he tore those skins up! With sweat dripping and muscles bulging, he seemed to be rolling those drums in another world, totally removed from us. Not only did Forest hear the beat of a different drummer, he *was* a different drummer, drumming out his own beat.

On many occasions Forest would pick my mind. He'd needle me with some philosophical or theological question and then let me roam around the files of my mind, bringing up whatever thought or idea I had tucked away long ago.

Finally, I extracted myself from his room with all its memories, and Faye and I left the house, heading the car onto the interstate for our trip to where our son was struggling for life. We were adrift on an uncharted sea, and we didn't know how seaworthy our ship would be. We had never been here before. As my mind surfed for channels of resource and strength—wondering if we had called everyone who needed to know and had touched all bases of support—a familiar statement by the apostle Paul to Timothy came into focus: "for I know whom I have believed, and am persuaded that he is able to keep that which I have committed unto him against that day" (2 Timothy 1:12 KJV).

New light dawned on that old Scripture verse. Paul seemed to say that *belief precedes knowledge*. But Paul's experience ("I know") validated his faith ("I have believed"). What once was faith became sure knowledge, based on his experience through crises. As the interstate wound its way through the softly rolling hills, Paul's declaration started cutting its way into my soul.

I had always believed that, with God's help, I could take whatever came down the road of my life. This had been my faith and my belief system. Now my faith would be tested. I didn't yet really know if my faith would hold. I had never experienced any crisis like this one. But Paul's testimony gave courage. I was on an unfamiliar road, facing a new frontier, where either knowledge would come through experience and validate faith or it wouldn't!

As darkness wrapped itself around us like a soft blanket, Paul's words resurfaced in the words of the old hymn, and for miles I sang the chorus in my mind:

But I know whom I have believed,
And am persuaded that he is able
To keep that which I've committed
Unto him against that day.

All I had now was faith. And I hoped it would be enough.

Chapter Two

Faye and I drove the two hours of interstate highway to Winston-Salem almost in silence. About the only conversation was when our silent prayers became too much to contain and we verbalized spontaneously. The tears were so hard to hold back, and at times we let them flow. We had solid hope that once at the medical center, Forest would be all right. Yet I knew he was hurt badly, and I had this gnawing fear that he was in deep trouble. I dreaded the doctor's report that would come later that night.

Once we arrived in the emergency room at North Carolina Baptist Hospital, a strange feeling came over me. Only months before, I had completed an unpublished novel in which, in one scene, the main character takes a member of his family to a medical center. Naturally, my description of the emergency room, doctors, and attendants was based on my familiarity with Baptist's facilities, since I had served on its board of directors.

Things started happening just about the way I had described them in the novel. The first person I called, after we talked with the doctor in charge, was the director of the medical center. He assured me that wheels were turning and that everything possible would be done for Forest. Then I called our friend L. L. McGee, a chaplain there. Even though it was about midnight, Mac came, embraced us, and was prepared to stay with us as long as needed.

All these incidents and persons (with fictitious names) were part of the novel. Even the private room off the emergency wing was as I had described it in the book. The scary thing—and I dared not mention any of this to Faye—was that my novel's main character ends up losing the member of his family. That thought would not go away. I had been too prophetic in the novel, and right there I determined never to write fiction again. Almost everything we experienced that night had been catalogued in my book over a year before. I wanted to rip my novel to shreds, hoping somehow that I could thus change what I feared would be the ending of the current drama.

In my clearer moments I knew that my novel had no impact on what was happening. Yet the sinister suggestion surfaced, as I leaned against the rails of the emergency room loading dock, hoping the fresh air of a cooling night would clear my brain: *Was some mysterious power moving my fiction to fact?* The thought persisted.

I later realized that I was but exercising in the laboratory of futility where many people, standing beside suffering loved ones, seek to identify themselves in the causes. Superstition is never far from our thoughts, and such flawed reasoning often leads us to assume that tragedies happen because of something we did or did not do. To be sure, the cause-and-effect principle does operate in life. But merely thinking negative thoughts about a loved one, or a situation involving a loved one, does not cause something bad to happen.

I recall the day when a car lost control and crashed against a stone wall at the edge of our front lawn. Fortunately, no one was hurt. But later Rachel, our younger daughter, came into my study sobbing. "Dad, I caused that accident," she said as she collapsed in my arms.

"You did what?" I asked.

"I made that wreck happen."

"How?"

Regaining some measure of composure, she said, "Well, I was bored. Nothing was happening. I thought to myself, *I wish something big and exciting would happen.* In less than ten minutes that poor man came barreling through our front lawn. He could have been killed. We could have been killed because we had just finished our football game out there. Oh, Dad," she cried. "I didn't mean to cause that. I didn't!"

During the next hour I had to convince our eleven-year-old that by thinking or wishing we cannot control the universe, not even our little part of it. Most things, in fact, are beyond our control. We do not cause them by writing or speaking about them. Yet in times of hurting and dying we often place ourselves in the driver's seat of events. Not only is this wrong reasoning, it is superstition that is counterproductive and dangerous if not corrected.

The short respite in the night air cleared my thinking, moving me from fiction to fact and faith. Prayer became an abiding exercise. I came to know what Paul meant by his exhortation to "pray without ceasing" (1 Thessalonians 5:17 KJV). I was never two sentences away from prayer all night. For days I prayed and prayed that Forest would be healed.

Prayer became an all-encompassing presence. Even as I spoke to people about subjects unrelated to Forest, prayer's presence never left me. It permeated my very being and saturated my soul. Every thought was laced in heart-cries lifted to God. Prayer became as much a part of me as breathing. At times my prayers were firm and demanding of God, and at other times they were pleading and begging. During those crucial hours prayer became the lifestyle of a voice crying in the wilderness.

I discovered that my prayers did not alter the facts, but they altered me. And that, I believe, is the very essence of prayer. Though prayer does not always change the circumstances, it changes us to deal with the circumstances. I experienced a power and strength I never knew I had and never thought possible. God was giving me a bulwark on which I could stand. Psalm 46 started making sense: "God is our refuge and strength, a very present help in trouble" (46:1 KJV). I was in trouble, and God was that "present help" I needed.

The psalmist continued outlining my experience: "Therefore will not we fear, though the earth be removed, and though the mountains be carried into the midst of the sea" (Psalm 46:2 KJV). My earth was being removed, and the mountains were disappearing. The circumstances were scary, but through the practice of unceasing prayer I was finding balance. And security. In this praying without ceasing I recalled yet another psalm's encouragement: "thou has founded a bulwark because of thy foes, to still the enemy and the avenger" (Psalm 8:2b RSV).

This bulwark became my fortress of security—at least for the moment. But as the night progressed, and turned into many nights and days, times came when I'd leave my fortress, venture outside God's security on my own, hoping that somehow I could effect change. Such actions are normal as one struggles to understand a land never before known or experienced.

My prayers took a practical turn as I prayed I could locate Becky in Chapel Hill. She had to know. Finally I was able to reach her and brief her as best as I could without pushing an alarm button. I then talked with her boyfriend and gave him a bit more information about the seriousness of Forest's condition. He said they would leave immediately to join us.

The resident physician in neurosurgery came to brief us. He was open and honest. You have a very sick son, we were told. The brain scan revealed numerous bruises on the brain. They would now drill a small hole in Forest's skull in which they would insert a little instrument to monitor brain pressure, the culprit that could cause the most damage. They would shave off some of his hair, he said, and I told him to take no more than necessary because Forest had a thing about his hair! He laughed, saying he'd be as careful as possible. I could hear Forest's first comment upon regaining con- sciousness: "Dad, don't let anybody in here to see me until this hair grows back." About four weeks before his accident he would hardly let his sister see him when extraction of four wisdom teeth doubled the size of his face, moving him to comment, "I look like a chipmunk with nuts in his jaws!"

The doctor had nearly finished his report when we heard foot- steps in the deserted hall outside our room. In walked Becky, followed by Dr. Tom Foster and Forest's longtime buddy Larry Phillips. I'll never forget the look on Larry's face—frustrated, hurt, scared. In his years as the associate pastor at Hickory's First Baptist Church, he had become close to Forest.

We asked the young physician to repeat his report, especially for Dr. Foster, a close friend, who we knew could support us better by having access to all available data. This time around, the doctor used medical terms for Dr. Foster's benefit. As they consulted on the case before them, they appeared to be speaking in an unknown tongue. When the report was over, we moved to the fourth-floor waiting room, just outside the intensive care unit where they had taken Forest.

Mac suggested that we all go up to his office on the fifth floor. And then the long vigil began. We asked Mac to lead us in prayer. He prayed a moving, comforting prayer, requesting healing for Forest and strength for us.

That was the longest night I've ever spent. But all the following nights were long, and so were the days. The doctors told us that Forest was not hurting, and for that we were grateful. I remembered how pain bothered him. Sometimes when he was sick he'd ask me to hold him, and he'd cry. Shedding tears never bothered Forest. He cried freely and frequently when he hurt. We never told him that "big boys don't cry." He learned that everybody ought to cry when they hurt; that's why God had given us tear ducts.

One time when he was catching on the baseball team, a foul ball hit him hard. I was standing close to the backstop and knew he was hurting. When the inning was over, he didn't go to the dugout but motioned for me to meet him behind the backstop. We moved farther back and sat down by ourselves. Then his tears started. "Dad, it hurts so bad. But I can't go out of the game. I'm the second batter up. What do I do?"

"If it hurts that bad, Son, take yourself out of the game," I urged him.

"No way. They need me, and I want to finish this game. Tell me what to do," he pleaded. The tears came, and he rolled in pain, motioning for me to help him take off his catcher's equipment.

"Okay," I said. "Go in there, swing at the first pitch, and hope for a fly ball or easy grounder that will get you out at first so you'll have the inning to recover."

And he did, but he hit the ball clear over the shortstop for a clean single. *Now you've done it,* I said to myself. But then the base umpire called time and pointed to Forest, and the coach sent in a runner to take his place.

"Why?" the plate ump yelled.

"He's their catcher," the base ump hollered back, and the plate ump nodded agreement and signaled for the pitcher to restart the game.

I eased toward the dugout, and Forest came to the fence, smiling, the pain seemingly gone.

"Nice hit," I smiled back.

"Yeah, thanks. Know what? I learned something up there. I'm going to start swinging at that first pitch from now on. With my low batting average they think I'll take that first pitch and then put it in there with only a little movement on it."

"Sounds logical," I agreed.

"Something else, Dad. I know you told me to hit for a quick out, but from the time I left you until I got to the plate I had another thought."

"Like what?"

"Like they always let the catcher have a runner in our league so he can get his equipment on and not hold up the game. So I asked God to let me get a hit. I really prayed about it while I waited in the on-deck circle. When I stood up there I had confidence, and I went for the first pitch. I just decided that the pain would be easier to handle if I got a hit. Like you've said, Dad, 'Nothing like success to ease the pain of getting success.'"

I wondered during those long hours of our first night whether the success of medical science was easing his pain. I hoped so. I prayed for that.

In a short time they let Faye and me go into his room. They prepared us for all the equipment they had hooked up to him, but maybe they had not prepared us well enough. I've never seen so many gadgets in all my life. He seemed to have tubes and wires running into every part of his body. His breathing was labored, and he thrashed about, holding my hand and squeezing. I didn't realize how big he was, filling up the entire bed with his feet pushing for more room.

The shock of seeing your loved one lying helpless is almost more than any human being can take. You want to do something. Anything. But you are helpless. You, a father or mother who has always been able to fix things for your child, have met your match. No gentle or firm word has any impact. The kiss or hug that always seemed to heal whatever was hurting has no power. You can only stand there, overwhelmed by what others are doing with their high technology but powerless to effect any progress yourself. No longer in control of anything, you turn from your child, wipe away your tears, and walk lonesomely into the half-lit hall, hoping and praying that somehow, sometime, someone will do something that you can't do but that must be done for your loved one.

Early on Monday morning, Dr. David Kelly, chief of the neuro-surgery service, carefully and candidly told us of the severity of Forest's injury. "We'll need a miracle," he said. "We'll need several miracles to pull Forest through this. He has fifty or sixty bruises all over his brain. Quite frankly," he said in deep thought, "his brain looks like the scan of a person who did not survive. A doctor viewing this scan, and not knowing the situation, would conclude he was looking at the report of an autopsy."

Though the physician's report was hard to take, I was grateful for his honesty. Sometimes families recoil from such honest infor-mation, yet in the long run, reality must be faced, and the sooner the better. Sugarcoating has no place in life-and-death situations, and this is also true as family members talk with each other during the ordeal. Facing reality is not giving up hope; it is placing hope in perspective. I discovered more about this as our vigil with Forest progressed. But for then, reality and hope were struggling for a place to stand in my muddled thinking.

As we tried to process that bit of gross reality, Dr. Kelly said, "One miracle you've already had—that he was not killed instantly. We will do our best, but we are not too hopeful at this point." We appreciated his honesty, but you can imagine how shaken we were. Words would not come. Finally I managed to thank him for his candor and assured him of our confidence in the ability of his team working to save our son's life.

"The one thing Forest has going for him," Dr. Kelly told us, "is his youth and strong body. He has taken care of himself, and in the long run that may be the only weapon he has."

I was grateful that Forest had been concerned about his body. I remembered the bodybuilding exercises he constantly engaged in—weight lifting, jogging, calisthenics, sports—his attention to proper food and rest, his decision not to smoke. We knew he'd need that strong body. *Now, God,* I prayed silently, *please do your part. Forest has done his. He's cared for the body you gave him like the temple it is. He's cultivated his soul along with his body. Please, God,* I pleaded, *help our son.*

By midmorning of that first day, dozens of friends started filling the waiting room, joining our vigil, lending their support, looking after our needs.

Faye and I had not slept or eaten much. Coffee and prayer had been our steady fare during that long night and longer morning. We tried to eat lunch, but food was tasteless and appetite was lost. About that time Perry and Kitty Crouch rushed in from Raleigh. "The reason we were not here earlier," Perry explained, "was that we learned the news only two hours ago, and it took us that long to drive here."

When I saw Dr. Crouch step off the elevator, a surge of strength came over me. Perry had headed North Carolina Baptists for twelve years and led the million-plus Baptists in their 3,500 churches to new heights of ministry. During his tenure as head executive of the state convention, I was pastor of Durham's First Baptist Church and had served on several committees that worked closely with Perry. He was my mentor and I his grateful student.

But it was not *that* relationship that stimulated energy in me at the sight of the aging servant of God, but rather knowing the valleys he had experienced in his own family. I knew he had spent many hours in the same waiting room where he was greeting us. In a four-year period, he had lost his first wife to cancer, his physician-son to a brain tumor, and his grandson in an airplane crash; and a granddaughter was then suffering from a lingering, incurable disease. Yet Perry Crouch never faltered. His faith had become stronger, and his life-view remained positive. Faye and I ran to meet them. Perry embraced me like his own son, and Kitty held Faye like her own daughter.

In a few minutes some of the gathered friends determined that Faye and I should go to the motel they had reserved and provided for us. "We can't leave Perry and Kitty," I protested.

"Well, take them with you to the room. But you two have got to get some rest," the group insisted.

In the motel room we talked and talked. The Crouches wisely let both of us ventilate our feelings without interrupting. They offered no theology, no blind-faith statements, no guilt-producing doctrines that people too often splash upon guilt-drenched and grief-soaked victims of loss. Both Perry and Kitty did exactly what we needed— they listened!

I had spent many years as a pastor listening to people, but I did not really know the power of listening. I'm sure we said many things that were off base, at least theologically, but never once did the Crouches confront us. They gave us comfort simply by being there and listening.

We talked long and intensely about Forest, his outlook on life, his faith, his leadership, his love for people. "Perry," I said, "Forest is not only my son—he's my buddy, my pal. Everything I've ever dreamed about in having a son he is. And double. I could not have ordered a custom-made son any more perfect than he is. I can't lose him; I cannot!" And the tears came in torrents.

Perry and Kitty sat silently, tears streaming to join our own. I don't know how long we rocked the room with our sobbing, but in a few minutes Faye asked Perry to pray. He did—a most moving, comforting prayer. He prayed for Forest's recovery and for the doctors working with him. But then he prayed, "Not our will, but your will be done." I didn't want him to say that! I was afraid of what God's will might be, and I didn't want God's will if it meant losing Forest. I was not ready to give up Forest. No way! But I had a premonition that that would happen. I recoiled from the possibility.

Asking that "God's will be done" is not easy. In the garden of Gethsemane shortly before Jesus faced his own death, he prayed that "this cup" would pass from him, that his cross-death would not happen. Luke records that Jesus prayed: "Father, if thou art willing, remove this cup from me; nevertheless not my will, but thine, be done" (Luke 22:39ff. RSV). This was not easy, not even for Jesus. There's a lot of pain and frustration between that semicolon separating what Jesus wanted and his "nevertheless" that turned the matter over to God. Luke writes that "being in an agony he prayed more earnestly; and his sweat became like great drops of blood falling down upon the ground."

Matthew and Mark record that Jesus had three sessions of prayer about his coming ordeal. Each time he prayed, "My Father, if it be possible, let this cup pass from me; nevertheless, not as I will, but as thou wilt" (Matthew 26:36ff. RSV; Mark 14:32ff. RSV). Praying such a prayer is no simple matter. Even after Jesus prayed the prayer he came back two more times, praying the same prayer.

I didn't want God's will; I wanted my will. And I believe that Jesus felt the same way in his bout with God in Gethsemane. Reaching the point of turning things over to God is never simple, no matter how much we lip-sync proper theology on the issue. On the thin pages of leather-bound Bibles it seems so logical and theological. But on the thick pavement of reality where we live our lives it's sticky. And "nevertheless your will, God," is the most choking phrase we dare try to utter, especially when it's contrary to what we really want.

Yet *nevertheless* is the most powerful word in the vocabulary of faith. In our grammar books it is known as a relative or conjunctive adverb. It connects two clauses; it relates two statements. And in the grammar of faith it is also a connector. It connects the believer to God. It connects our weakness to God's power and purpose for us.

But when life was caving in for me, no such theological perspective surfaced, mainly because I was not ready. Some things I had to work through, just as did my Lord in his three-time effort to accept God's will.

I dared not voice my resentment at Perry's prayer about God's will. Such feelings were best unexpressed. He was right, but the time was not right for me. A big jungle lay before me. I had to work through that vine-infested real estate before I could pray Jesus' nevertheless prayer.

The Crouches sat in the uncomfortable motel chairs and encouraged us to lie down, just to rest if nothing else. In a few minutes I heard Faye breathing the breath of sleep—she always could go to sleep before anyone else! But sleep wouldn't come to me. I could feel my whole body tensing, just waiting for the phone to ring.

Every time I would almost go under, I'd jerk up and look at the silent phone that I swore I had heard ring.

R. F., I said silently to myself, *this can't go on. This is only Monday afternoon, the first day, and the doctors said we would be in for a long pull—days, weeks, maybe months. You will be bug crazy if you keep this up. Your stomach is already in knots, your hands are shaking like a loose leaf in the wind, and your mind is simply not functioning rationally. Something's got to give, or you'll never make it.*

I turned on my stomach, pulled the pillow over my head, and tried to pray, but nothing was happening. Then, almost as if watching a movie or an animated painting, I saw Abraham with his son Isaac, struggling to get up a briar-covered hill. The Old Testament story came to mind in vivid strokes. And like an artist working on canvas, my mind started painting pictures of that centuries-old incident.

I recalled that Abraham had prayed for a son. In his old age God had granted his request, giving him his only son, Isaac. With Isaac's birth, God promised Abraham that he would become the father of many nations, that his descendants would cover the earth like sand on the beach.

Then God told Abraham to offer Isaac as a sacrifice on an altar of worship. In Old Testament times human sacrifice was quite common. So the command to offer Isaac was not utterly strange, insofar as the act of human sacrifice was concerned. But it did rattle Abraham that God, after giving him just one son and making all those promises, should now direct him to sacrifice that son.

Abraham prepared the altar, tied down his son, and had raised the knife to take Isaac's life when an angel appeared and commanded: "Don't you touch him! God knows now you trust him. Over there in the bushes is a ram; use it for your sacrifice."

As I lay there, with Abraham and Isaac standing in bold relief in my mind's eye, I knew what I had to do. I had to be Abraham with *my* son!

I had never totally given Forest to God, though in most ways I had. We had dedicated him when he was a baby; had reared him in the nurture and admonition of the Lord as our faith directed; had given him guidance in spiritual matters. Those things we had done. And he had taken our teaching and training seriously. God was very real to Forest.

But there was one area of his life I had not committed to God. I did not want him to be a minister! Even though I had spent decades in the ministry, I did not want my son to follow me. I had wanted to be a lawyer, but God had called me into the ministry. I accepted his call and have known many years of fulfillment, but maybe there was always a part of me that God didn't have in the ministry. Many times I fought like a rebel with a cause; other times I fought like a rebel *without* a cause. For the past two years I had been in another type of ministry—in industry, in the marketplace. Market Ministry Inc., we called our organization, which was designed "to help people in making a living to make living worthwhile."

I had told Forest two weeks before his accident that I was going back to the pastorate. He was happy about the decision, and I was happy. Still, I did not want him to be a pastor. He, like me, had planned to be a lawyer and go into politics. He carried on his key ring an official trinket from the United States Senate, and told me that one day he'd be there and would give trinkets to his supporters as the senator had given one to him.

I don't really know how many of Forest's plans were an extension of my dreams and how many were genuine convictions on his part. I sensed, though, that he was responding to his own genuine feeling of vocational calling, not mine. He was influenced by me in many things, but on the biggies he went his own way, listening to the beat of his own drums. He had a keen way of sorting out the options before him and choosing his own style and path. Yet, as he had implied in the essay completed only hours before his accident, "This is my dream on paper now." He left the door open in case God had something else for him to do.

As I lay there trembling, I prayed silently. *God, I've never given Forest completely to you. Father, I'm not sure that one person can give another to you, not even a father his son. But I've got to let you know that I want your will for Forest's life. If you want him to be a minister, that's what I want. God, he'll make a better minister than I have been or could ever be. If that's what you want, spare his life,*

and I'll do everything I can to stay out of your way with him. I'll
even encourage him to be a pastor, if that's what you want, God.
I'll even give my life so he can live. Father, if one of us must die, let
it be me. You'll be a lot better off in the deal. Forest has more on
the ball than I have. He'll do you a better job than I could ever do.
Please spare him. If somebody's got to go, let me be the ram.

God, I concluded my silent prayer, *you have me totally; you have*
my only son totally. I'm turning everything over to you. You know
what I want, but you also know more—you know what's best. Not
my will, but thine be done.

A peace came over me that I cannot explain. The trembling
stopped, my stomach relaxed, and my mind stopped spinning. I
turned over on my left side and immediately went to sleep.

A few hours later I got up refreshed. "I want to tell you what's
happened," I said to Faye and the Crouches. Then I told them I had
"Abrahamed" my son. "I don't know what all this means," I said.
"But I now have peace."

Actually, the peace I felt came from a session of bargaining with
God, one of the several stages in processing grief. Prophets and
saints alike went through that stage when crises and tragedies came.
It's part of the process, and I was no different.

Bargaining with God is simply, and often profoundly, trying to
work out a deal with God. "God, you do this and I'll do that. You'll
get what you want and I'll get what I need." As I look back on what
happened in that motel room, I recognize I offered God a deal! Let
me hasten to clarify: what I did then was real and sincere—I was
dealing with all my cards on the table.

My peace, felt so deeply the moment I offered Forest to God,
came from my "deal." I really thought a bargain had been struck. I
believed there'd be a ram in the bushes, and I was even willing to
be the ram. In my saner theological moments I know that God does
not operate in some smoke-filled back room. But when your loved
one is suffering and maybe dying, you don't think theologically or
logically. You go for any port in the storm. All your childhood
fantasies and misguided views of God you thought you'd laid to
rest are suddenly resurrected and take on a life of their own.

My "nevertheless, God, your will be done" was actually based on the bargain I thought I'd struck with God. Bargaining with God is normal and natural. That we bargain (or try to) is healthy; it enables us to proceed through the other stages, such as *denial* ("This is not happening!"); *anger* ("Why did this happen to me?"); *acceptance* ("It did happen."); and *writing new chapters* ("My life is not over yet.").

Although bargaining with God does not result in a deal, the *process* is not fruitless. What I did was real and was needed in my life. And it would become therapeutic for me as I processed the grief that lay ahead.

Chapter Three

As Labor Day Monday turned to Tuesday, we still hoped for a ram in the bushes. Family and friends from all over the state came to offer support. The telephone in the intensive care waiting room was seldom silent.

Dr. Ralph Scales, president of Wake Forest University and a close friend, made early contact with us. As a member of the university's board of trustees, I had worked closely with him for many years. In a hand-delivered letter he assured me that the entire resources of the university were at our disposal. The Reverend Henry Stokes, a staff member at Wake Forest, brought the letter, indicating he was there for the duration to meet any need we had. He was a Godsend. In a gentle style saturated with keen insight and understanding, he monitored our needs with delicate sensitivity. Henry immediately assumed the duty of phone-call screener. "You can't take every call," he reminded us. "You will drain yourself simply by talking with well-meaning friends."

And he was right. One of the most exhausting experiences is constantly talking with friends about the situation. You go over the same data with each new contact. Every phone call was appreciated, but each one added weight even as the caller sought to share the burden. Oftentimes one hungers for solitude, longing for respites that come too seldom when crisis throws its heavy cloak about one's shoulders.

I strongly urge families to find a good balance between being available and unavailable in times of extreme pain and stress. A person cannot accommodate every gesture of support and kindness that comes in a crisis. Having someone screen calls diplomatically is imperative. The more traumatic the crisis, the more people seek

out the family to offer support. While such kindness is commendable and appreciated, it can wear out the family.

Henry knew what calls to put through. One call came from
Congressman James T. Broyhill, later Senator Broyhill, a friend
since childhood. "I just called to let you know we are thinking about
you and praying for Forest," Jim said, but I could hardly hear him
for the background noise at his end of the phone line.

"Jim, where are you? What's going on? Sounds like you are in
the middle of a circus," I said.

He chuckled softly. "That could be. I'm just off the floor of
Congress. I can't leave the floor, so they got this phone for me from
someplace. I just had to hear your voice and let you know that
several of us in Congress prayed for Forest at breakfast this morning."

Another call came from the Billy Graham team, letting us know
that they had had a special prayer meeting for Forest. Ann Graham
Lotz and her husband, Dr. Danny Lotz, had been members of our
church in Durham and had informed the team of the situation.

Many calls came from high school students and faculty advisors
from across the South. Forest was president of the Hickory High
School student council as well as president of the Southern Association of Student Councils, which encompassed fifteen states. The
annual meeting of the Southern Association was scheduled for
October, and Forest had been instrumental in bringing the large
convention to Hickory. He and the Hickory student group were deep
in plans for the meeting, which was only a month away.

Word soon spread of Forest's accident and his struggle for life.
The Hickory press reported daily on his progress. Calls came from
all over the country, especially from students in the association's
fifteen states, to let us know that special prayer meetings were being
held for his recovery. Students from around the state came by the
hospital to visit, offer support, and mingle their tears with ours.

Some family and friends came and, like Henry Stokes, stayed
for the duration. We came to know the meaning of "support systems." Though constant conversation drains energy and must be
carefully monitored, without the presence and touch of caring
friends, we never would have survived. Some of the most effective

support was from people who simply came, spoke, and sat, sometimes for hours, without the need to engage us in conversation. Just
a smile at the right time, or a hand laid gently on the arm, became
genuine support. Establishing a workable rhythm between accepting too much support and too little is a delicate challenge. But it
must be handled; otherwise support becomes counterproductive.

By Thursday we knew that there would be no ram in the bushes.
The medical team told us that even if Forest should live, he would
not be the person we had known and loved for nearly eighteen years.
"There's too much damage to his brain," they told us, and we
interpreted that to mean that his life would have little or no quality.

At that point Faye, Becky, Rachel, and I had a private meeting.
We reviewed the information given us by the doctors. Nothing they
projected was good. "Dad," Becky said, "I cannot bear to see
Brother lie there like that for weeks, maybe months, on life-support
systems. They've got enough stuff in there to machine his life
forever." Rachel agreed. She added few words, but she didn't have
to. Her big eyes, inherited from my mother, were always bright,
laughing. Now they were dull and sad.

Faye listened intently, as was always her style and gift in relationships. Finally, she spoke, and would later confide to her diary:
"Mothers have a special touch and feeling with their children. The
baby grows close to her heart so she can protect and love him deeply
even before birth—and feed him, too. The feeding continues and
gets to be a bigger task as he reaches teenage years," and a little
smile played on her lips, remembering no doubt the four, not three,
meals needed for Forest daily. "We love Forest deeply, and what
I'm going to say hurts deeply, but from all we've learned from the
doctors we now know Forest stands no chance of recovering and
being who he was." Her flowing tears cast her vote with her
daughters.

"Dad, what do you say? What do you think?" Becky asked.

At that moment words—my stock-in-trade, the lifeline of my
ministry and profession, the very essence of who I am as a person
and pastor—were not there, failing me at the most crucial time in
my life: the life-death decision for my only son. I don't know how

long the deadening silence lasted, broken only by a family's soft sobbing. It seemed an eternity.

Finally, the words formed. "Girls," I said, speaking more to my daughters than my wife. "When you were little you were confronted more with death than your peers because I was always conducting funerals. You'd ask me, 'Why did So-and-So die?' I never had good answers for that childhood question until one day I heard my dad speak about his neighbor: 'He was so sick he just died.' I edited that idea a bit and told you that 'Mr. So-and-So died because he was too sick to live.'

"I think that's what's going on now with Forest—he's too sick to live. There's a difference between living and existing. Forest is only existing now. If we can prolong his life, we must. But I don't think that's an option."

Over the years I have ministered to families whose loved ones were fumbling with the thin curtain that separates life from death. I have watched them debate whether to "pull the plug" or insert more plugs. As carefully and delicately as possible, I tried to clarify the issue for them, reminding them that the question was not, "Shall we prolong life or shorten life?" but rather, "Shall we prolong death or shorten the dying?"

In such times the debate revolves around the quality of life versus the quantity of life. What if the body can endure but the brain cannot? Does one imprison the mind in the clutches of a body that functions only through the efforts of high-tech enablers? When the quality of life is gone, for whose purposes are more plugs inserted—the patient's or the family's? One physician properly corrected me when I asked, "Shall we pull the plug?" He said, "It's not so much a matter of pulling plugs as allowing nature to take its course." He was right. There comes a time in many situations when only machines are alive, not the patient. At such times the humane and moral course of action is to leave nature alone.

Now it was my turn to see if my philosophy, given so freely to others, would fit and work for me and my family.

We talked some more and cried a lot more in that session, but the bottom line never changed. We decided, individually and collectively, that there are many things worse than death, and having

Forest exist in a vegetative state would be one of those "worse things." We did not have the choice of prolonging his life or shortening his life; our only option was to delay his death and prolong his dying. Making that decision was the most difficult thing we had ever done.

Together we told the medical personnel that they should not attempt any heroics. Keep him comfortable, but use no life-sustaining machines, we said. They nodded understanding and may have asked for my signature—I can't remember. At any rate, the decision was made; the deed was done. Forest's days were numbered—at least we hoped the time was days, not months. Some families in the waiting room had kept vigil for months as their loved ones lay comatose.

From this point on, the content of our prayers changed. We had prayed earnestly that God would heal Forest; that he would bring him out of the coma, restore him physically, and generally rehabilitate him to his pre-accident condition. Now the thrust of our prayers went from "heal him" to "take him"—take him to that "place not made with hands, eternal in the heavens" where he could get on with living.

The essence of prayer, too often praised by most of us rather than practiced, became a living reality in our lives. I had often preached on prayer, reminding my listeners that God answers all prayers with one of four options: *Yes, No, Wait,* and *What?* We had wanted God's Yes to our petitions for Forest's healing, but medical evidence revealed God's No. For two or three days we fantasized that God's Wait was in gear. But as negative medical evidence mounted, we soon discovered that God's No was solid; to have contended further with God could have produced his What?

When I first ventured publicly that God's fourth answer is What? some thought their pastor a bit irreligious until I explained. One day a young mother requested that I pray she would have a son since she already had two daughters. "Please pray for a little boy," she pleaded. She was six months pregnant! Had I dared such a prayer, I'm sure God would have yelled, "What?" Sometimes our prayers are as far-out as the young mother's request. I believe that God's

What? is not off target as a legitimate answer to prayers that ignore realities or transgress God's established order of the universe.

Given the evidence on medical scans and X-rays, plus the expert experience of a crack medical team, I think God's answer would certainly have been, What? And he might well have added: "Can't you see what's going on with Forest? Look at the evidence. More than fifty bruises on his brain. Get real." His simple No was enough; we dared not risk his What?

Risking God's What? is not a breach of faith; nor does it signal a lack of intelligence. I'm sure I've experienced God's What? many times. We are invited to "take everything to God in prayer," as the old hymn suggests. But prayers based on unreality do not allow reality to come into focus and may delay appropriate praying that asks for strength and courage to face the inevitable. At this point we knew Forest could not live, given the extent of his injuries. Facing that reality enabled us to start praying for courage to face circumstances we could neither control nor change.

With our decision made and communicated to the medical staff, we asked that our family and friends who had gathered around us adjourn to a special room the hospital had made available to us. As some twenty or more of us sat around a long conference table, I suggested that we join hands and asked my good friend Randall Lolley to lead our prayers. Dr. Lolley was then-president of Southeastern Baptist Seminary of Wake Forest. We had been classmates at Southeastern, and I had served on his board of trustees. He and his wife, Lou, had joined Faye and me on many holidays and vacations. Randall and I had roomed together for several years while serving on the Southern Baptist Convention's executive committee. He had become the brother I never had.

Randall's heart was breaking along with ours, but he was equal to the task. He held my left hand and started praying. Now Randall is tremendously energetic, almost hyper at times. He started praying a most beautiful and comforting prayer and unconsciously rubbing my thumb in a circular motion, constantly alternating between clockwise and counterclockwise. The harder he prayed, the harder he rubbed my thumb. Soon the pain of my thumb was catching up with the pain of my soul. When he had finished, I immediately stuck my thumb in my mouth for relief. "What's wrong?" he asked. "My thumb, Rand, my thumb. You about rubbed that sucker raw." And levity settled comfortably over the teary-eyed gathering, bringing us back to the human level we needed so desperately.

Even now, some eighteen years later, every time I rub my thumb I remember Randall and the prayer.

"God," he intoned, "we don't really know what to pray for. We've asked for healing, and you don't seem inclined that way. So what we really need is for you to do what is best for Forest. And if that means taking him to be with you totally, that's *not* okay because we want him to stay with us. But if you say that's the way it's going to be, then give us the strength to say that's okay with us if you will give us the strength to deal with it. But, Lord, don't let him linger on, suspended between life and death. Release him, Lord, release him. Turn him loose and let him go into whichever world you've decided. Please."

This time I was more open to "not my will but thine be done." On Monday I could not pray that prayer. But after I had "Abrahamed" my son, studied the medical evidence, and struggled in my Gethsemane, I could finally pray the prayer of Jesus the night before his cross.

The steady stream of family and friends grew as we approached the weekend. Stephen Shoemaker and Alan Sassar came as soon as possible to add their support. Both young men had been on the church staff in Durham as pastoral interns during their student days at Southeastern, some twenty miles away. As single roommates, our home became their home, and our children became their younger siblings. Every Sunday after worship they would hang around as Faye and I pulled things together to head home. Finally, Faye would say, "You guys got any lunch plans?" The answer was always the same, "No," and the forlorn faces of two twenty-somethings were more than Mother Faye could stand. "Come on by," she'd say, and they'd disappear immediately and be sitting in the driveway of our Roxboro Road home when we arrived.

Alan and Steve endeared themselves to our children, constantly giving them attention and playing with them, and they became excellent role models for each child. Soon after Sunday lunch, a game of touch football would develop on the lawn. "Give me two children and Tipper and we'll stand you," I would challenge. Tipper was the second of three German shepherds to find a big place in our hearts and home. "That's not fair," they both complained. "There's no way to catch a long pass with that German shepherd nibbling at your bottom," Steve argued. But all arguments to the contrary, Tipper was part of the deal and stayed in the game as my best defender.

I had mentored Alan and Steve in several ways, I guess, but in none more important to me at that moment than the hospital experience they gained on our visits to Duke Medical Center in Durham. Now, as pastors in their own right, they were applying their pastoral and personal skills on one who had had some part in training them. As I watched them move around among our family, offering skilled care, my heart was bursting with gratitude. I reflected on what life is all about—mentoring, passing on the torch, one generation instructing another, and then the instructed generation ministering to the mentors.

At times during my wilderness wanderings outside the intensive care unit, I could back off and observe various dynamics at work. I saw the church living out my favorite definition for it: "a hospital for souls where we alternately serve as patient and physician." There were times when I moved from patient to physician as I listened to other weary and teary pilgrims keeping vigil for their loved ones in the same unit. Maybe the healing I ultimately experienced had its genesis there as I shared with others and allowed them to share with me. Perhaps healing begins in the sharing. I discovered that reality in the months and years ahead. But just now I reverted to being the patient, and the hurting surfaced with force.

The medical staff gave us free rein in the intensive care unit. "You can see Forest as often as you like," the doctor offered. And we did. We talked with him constantly, especially since they told us that hearing is the last thing to go. "He may hear you even though he shows no response," we were told.

In later years I learned the truth of this theory. One day I drove some distance to visit a church member in an intensive care unit. The nurse told me my visit would have no meaning because the woman was completely comatose. I reckoned I'd go in after having driven some forty miles to see her. I entered the unit and discovered that she was indeed unconscious. Tubes and wires were running everywhere into her body. I placed my hand on her head, prayed, and quietly slipped out. Two weeks later she regained consciousness. Her first words to her daughter were, "Nancy, Dr. Smith came to see me and caught me with my teeth out!"

That incident made me glad that we had talked with Forest constantly during his last days. I don't know if he knew we were there or not, but I have the satisfaction of knowing that if he did hear us, he knew how much we loved and cared for him. That's what we told him—daily, even hourly.

Even after we had reached our decision not to prolong Forest's death, and had altered the objective of our prayers from "heal him" to "take him," the temptation to embrace any shred of hope continued. On one visit to Forest's room the nurse smiled and said, "Guess what? He peed," and high-fives were given all around. I dashed out to tell family and friends that something was going on and it looked good. I almost shouted for the whole hospital hall to hear, "Forest peed!"

About that time Dr. Mark Gulley came around the corner and asked me what the celebration was about. "The nurse said Forest peed this morning," I told him. I could tell the prominent psychiatrist was not impressed. His lips curled in a forced smile, but behind his deep brown eyes I saw something I had seen many times before when some of my ideas were off-the-wall. Mark was one of my pastors, "the priest at my elbow" as another friend put it. Our friendship had deepened over the years as Mark generously accepted the role of pastor into which our family had cast him.

Mark put his hand on my shoulder, gently turned me around, and headed us back to Forest's room. I could tell by his muted body language that he was about to set me straight on something. Slowly, but with firmness, Mark said, "R. F., one pee does not a cure make."

"But, Mark," I argued. "He is also squeezing my hand. When I say, 'Forest, can you hear me?' he squeezes my hand. He did that with his mother and with Becky and Rachel, too."

"Have you asked him *not to squeeze* your hand if he hears you?" Mark pushed the issue.

"Well, no," I admitted.

"Then let's go do that," he suggested.

Sure enough, when I said anything to Forest, he squeezed my hand.

Mark explained. "That involuntary muscle reaction could be brought on by a number of causes, perhaps even the medication being administered."

As carefully and tenderly as he could, Mark made me face the reality of Forest's impending and inevitable death, helping me to give up the false hope that had wriggled into my rational thinking. Hope is a basic ingredient of life, without which life becomes a formless mass of dreams and plans. But hope contending in the face of hard data to the contrary is not hope; it is fantasy.

Some years later I read on the T-shirt of our church's parking lot attendant, *Now that I have given up hope I am at peace.* I chided my good friend about his apparent bad theology. But I've come to appreciate the unknown author's insight. What is "given up" is not hope but fantasy masquerading as hope. And once we give up the fantasy, there is a peace. The peace that comes from facing reality strips away our need to pretend or to scour around for proof that we are faithful.

A wife told me after two years of separation from her husband, "I had hoped we would make the marriage work. But now I realize such hoping was mere pretending. It was not going to work. Once I accepted that reality, I found a peace that's enabling me to work positively in another direction."

Sometimes religious people make such fantasized hope a badge of faith. To say "All hope is gone" is a surrender to fatalism, they feel. So they look under every rock and behind every tree for some shred of hope that will prove their faithfulness. But such a process delays healing because it denies reality. There comes a time when one must say, "This is how it is. I cannot pretend otherwise. I don't need to prove anything." When such discovery is recognized, healing begins. In the years ahead I had many occasions to pass on

Mark Gulley's ministry of reality to families outside intensive care units who would reach for fantasy and call it hope.

Chapter Four

Football games in the heart of the Atlantic Coast Conference were in full swing the second weekend of September. In Winston-Salem, Wake Forest was hosting the University of Virginia. Some seventy miles east of our vigil, N.C. State, the University of North Carolina, and Duke were playing, and many people stopped by on their way to or from the games to express concern and offer support.

The University of Virginia football team was quartered at the motel where we were staying. On Friday evening during one of my respites from the hospital, I stood outside our room and watched as big, strapping, healthy young men about the age of my son milled around psyching up for tomorrow's gridiron battle with my alma mater.

My pain deepened as I looked at those young men—full of life, so much future ahead of them, so many years of growth and fun and love. One day they would marry, have children, perhaps name them for their dads. But I knew, in those painful, pensive moments, that no such future was mine or my son's.

People who claim that tears of grief are only "for ourselves" are only half-right. I believe we also grieve over the future our loved ones will miss and what we will miss without their presence. The younger the loved one, the more the feeling of loss of the future. The feeling that the person died before he or she ever lived is common. I often hear the expression, "What a waste!" Indeed. The regrets for "what might have been" hang heavy and are never finally or fully assuaged.

I walked toward some older men standing around with the younger men—coaches, I guessed. I spoke, commented on the refreshing evening air, and wished them luck on the morrow. Then added, "But not too much luck; you're playing my school." They allowed as how they understood my loyalty, and guessed I would be at the game. I could not share the "game" I was in, so I just lied and said, "Yeah." I went to my room, closed the door, and cried over what could never be for me and my son.

There's a special relationship between father and son, just as there is between father and daughter. But there's no door that's closed to a dad and his son. When the door states emphatically "Men Only," the father and son march bravely through it, no questions asked, no quarter given. They know they have so much in common that no law or tradition can limit their togetherness.

When Forest was born at North Carolina Memorial Hospital on the campus of the University of North Carolina in Chapel Hill on November 10, 1960, I shall never forget the feeling I experienced when the doctor emerged through those forbidding doors to declare, "Congratulations, Pastor. You've got a son!"

No words can ever describe the emotion that saturated my being as the news sank in. I could hear baseball bats cracking, basketballs bouncing in one-on-one battles, workshop tools whirring, finely tuned cars roaring in restored engines, and solid wood powering golf balls down fairways.

"Wow," I yelled softly as the nurse brought the newborn through the doors for my first glimpse of the son who'd bear my name as Robert Forest Smith III. He was so proud of that name, worn also by his grandfather, whose talent for music and woodwork he inherited. He always signed his full name, giving the *III* a flourish. He reminded us often that the future of the Smith line rested with him. "Be good to me," he cautioned when finding himself in some tight spot with me. "I hold the future of your name in my custody," he'd tease.

As I lay on the motel bed I knew the line was ending. Until now, no doors had ever barred our entrance together. But soon he would go through a door that only he could enter. I would have to stand outside as spectator, not unlike the many times I had sat in the stands at his ball games, watching as squeeze plays were executed. And I knew the big guy running from third base to home would do everything in his power to knock my catcher-son out of the way, out of the play. All I could do was pray he would not be hurt.

Now I prayed Forest's hurt was not hurting him. The line would soon end. We were ready if not prepared. I doubt that we are ever prepared for the death of a loved one. Oh, we get ready. We watch them linger, oftentimes suffering intense pain, and we pray for their release. We are ready for their departure, but we are never prepared.

Monday night, September 11, the vigil continued. Now in the eighth day of a journey whose strangeness was weirdly becoming too familiar, we wondered how many miles we had yet to travel.

Faye confessed to me that she could no longer bear to visit Forest. "I want to go in one more time and tell him goodbye," she said. "I don't think it will be much longer." Her voice trailed off as she made her way down the hall.

Standing beside his bed for the last time, the mother who had brought him into the world, then brought the world to him, was bidding farewell as he prepared to take his leave.

As this book was in process, Faye described for me this last visit with her son. She stood at his bed and rubbed his arms and legs—long legs and arms she had felt pushing and kicking in her womb not yet eighteen years ago. With tenderness in her soft Southern accent she told her son how much she loved him, that she hoped he was not hurting, how proud she was of him, and how much she would miss him. In her own special way, and as only a mother can, she gave him permission to leave us.

In the years ahead I would recall how important it is for family to give the loved one permission to die, to exit their family circle. As pastor I encourage the family to grant such permission. For many reasons, some cannot perform the task. So I ask them if they are ready to give permission. When they agree, I have a prayer in which I convey the family's permission. I'm amazed at how many times the loved one departs shortly after permission to leave is granted.

Faye's permission was delivered, and she left the room. "I'm okay now," she said. "I have had my time with my son. Let's go to the motel."

Surrounded by friends, we prepared to leave the intensive care unit sometime after midnight had ushered in September 12. Chaplain Mac McGee offered escort to our car. Just as we exited the main doors of Baptist Hospital, I heard Larry Phillips and Alan Sassar fairly yell for us. We turned around and walked back to meet my two former associates now out of breath from running through the sprawling hospital.

"It's over," Larry said. And Alan nodded his head as all five of us embraced and let the tears flow.

We made our way back to the waiting room on the fourth floor that had become an eight-day wilderness in which we had learned much and suffered more.

As the fellow pilgrims gathered around us, I fell to my knees. That's when I told God to get in his Black Chair. "Sit down, God . . . I'm angry, I'm hurting, and I need to talk." I had some things I needed to say.

And I did!

"God," I shouted. "Is this what we get for serving you? Forest loved you so much. His whole life was built around you. Around serving you. Around living for you. You were able to touch lives through him you'd touched in no other way. He was the best reflection of you I've ever seen. Why in the name of all that's holy did you allow this to happen? Why didn't you fix it? Have you no real power? Have you no real love? Kids all over this town are strung out on drugs, with no present that's worth a hoot, and no future anyone would dare bet on. But Forest was everything you could have wanted. Why him? Why our son? If this is what you are all about, then I've missed the boat somewhere."

No voice answered me. On and on I railed against the Most High God. But he was silent. Like Job, I wanted God to say something—anything, just so long as he spoke.

The silence of God is mute testimony that God's a good listener. I believe God allows us opportunity for ventilation of anger because expression of anger is predicated on a relationship and, too, anger is but the flip side of love. Anger is love confused or hurt, especially in our relationship with God. One does not get angry—really angry—with a person who doesn't count, who doesn't have significant impact on one's life. Sometimes the stronger the relationship, and the deeper the love, the more intense the anger.

I daresay God maintains silence for the same reason we often do not speak when a friend is angry—"You can't tell her anything right now. She's too angry. Let her get it out of her system, and then we'll talk."

Perhaps another reason for God's silence is that we are in no position to accept what God would say. Some years ago a friend of mine was working on his doctoral dissertation. His professor noted that his bibliography did not include works by certain German theologians.

"But," my friend protested, "those works are not translated into English."

"So?" mused the professor.

"I don't know German."

"Well, then," observed the prof, "you'd best make plans to learn German."

The professor and student had gone as far as they could go until the student worked his way to a new level. The student disciplined himself to learn German; then he and his mentor went on with their project.

Sometimes God cannot speak to us until we are prepared to listen. We must reach a different level. I'm convinced that God's silence is not arbitrary or designed to "teach us a lesson." Rather, what God would say cannot be understood or appropriated by us until we have worked our way to a new level of perception.

I don't know how long I knelt on that cold floor. Then I stopped, and was as silent as the God against whom I had stormed. The quietness was interrupted only by the soft sobbing of Faye and others who witnessed my Black Chair session with God. Finally, I felt relief, something of an emptiness, maybe the feeling a mother has when her baby is birthed. I was drained. My whole body was full of perspiration that would not sweat out. I knew something was over and something was being born. As friendly hands reached to help me up from my altar of pain, I knew the *evening of death* had ended. The *night of grief* had come. Ready or not, prepared or not, a new wilderness—or was it but a movement to the next level of the same wilderness?—was upon us. And with it came new experiences we had not even dreamed about in our most pessimistic and realistic modes.

Ezekiel had not even admitted there was a night, let alone confessed what happened to him during that darkness. God spoke to Ezekiel, asking him to sacrifice his expression of personal sorrow on the altar of public service, something that's often required of leaders, especially in times of national crises. He was a prophet of God instructed to allow his personal sorrow to become an example to God's people who were standing on the threshold of a national catastrophe. God told him to "sigh, but not aloud" (Ezekiel 24:17 RSV). God knew Ezekiel's pain but asked him not to express it "aloud."

So there was a night, even for the servant of God whose private grief was not allowed expression. He *did* have his night, however he handled it.

Like Ezekiel, we felt the night in all of its blackness. But unlike Ezekiel, we were not asked to withhold expression of our sorrow. It was night, heavy night. The night of our worst nightmares. We had lost our only son, our daughters their only brother, his grandparents their grandson. It was night.

Early on when Forest's death appeared inevitable, we suggested an autopsy. The one regret we have is that we did not donate his organs, but that was before the public was made aware of the opportunity and before the populace at large was sensitive to the possibilities of organ donation. I would like to think that somewhere someone had his eyes, his heart, and all other organs some suffering person could have used.

But that night I could think of only one thing—my son was gone. I, who had basked in the accolades that had come his way in such a short lifetime and was so proud of him, was without my boy, my pal.

The reality of routine soon set in. We had to check out of the motel. We had two cars there, and neither of us was in condition to drive the seventy miles home. My son had just died, and society expected me to be concerned with mundane things like motel rooms and driving cars. The anger expressed so recently toward God was about to be directed toward life's routines.

Two friends offered to drive us home. With that settled, and the cars packed, we began our journey together in separate cars, a symbol of the way we'd have to deal with Forest's death in the days and months ahead—*together but separately.* There's a real sense in which being together but separate is a basic principle in dealing with the pain of grief. In dealing with every experience there are two components: *working alone* and *working not alone.*

While sharing with people is tremendously important in the grief process, one must deal with the situation as a lone pilgrim on a quest for personal resolution. Sometimes you must simply back off from everyone and look deeply into your soul and discover what God is trying to reveal to you.

Every person is different, and this is never more true than when we are dealing with grief. What works for one person does not work for another. Though there may be common steps in dealing with loss and grief, each person weaves and tailors the garment that will fit and give warmth according to personal traits and talents. Faye and I shared our grief, but there were times when being alone in our separate worlds was important and necessary. By working alone, we could identify our special needs and seek ways to meet them. Then we would come together, share what we had discovered in our soul-ing times, and allow the other to take what could be personally appropriated.

So we left the scene of our greatest tragedy and headed for home. As my driver got our car up to full speed on I-40 in the lonely hours of Tuesday morning, I slumped down in the seat, completely exhausted. I could not sleep, but the tires, rolling effortlessly it seemed on the white ribbon of concrete, became a symphony of background music that gave security simply by their consistency in sound.

Then I started to notice glaring lights almost on our bumper. "What's going on back there?" I asked Anne, a close family friend whose vigil and friendship had been most supportive.

"I think we have a flirt driving an eighteen-wheeler," she said. "I guess he thinks I'm a lonely girl riding by myself." With that bit of information, I sat up so the driver could see me. He immediately slowed down, lowered his lights, and backed off. "Cool," said Anne. "Thanks."

I mumbled something, then slumped down again in my more comfortable position. It occurred to me that my slump was close to the fetal position. That said something about me, and something about the night of grief I had just entered. But then I started thinking about that trucker. *How dare he invade my grief? I've just lost my son, and he's trying to flirt with my friend out here on the interstate at three o'clock in the morning. The nerve of that nerd!*

I was experiencing what I had known all during my ministry: when death comes into a family, time stops. Life freezes in frames of reality-not-yet-recognized. The Greeks would understand the syndrome. They would say that *chronos* becomes *kairos. Chronos* means point of time, like 3:00 A.M., Tuesday, September 12, 1978. But *kairos* means season of time, like spring, summer, fall, winter. And kairos means death-time. The season of death. The night of grief.

The truck driver had just illustrated to me that while I had entered kairos, the rest of the world was on chronos. When you are in kairos it's hard to appreciate the world's chronos. People still tell jokes and laugh. They take their kids to school. Forest's classmates would answer the school bell even while the church bell tolled for him.

Life stands still in kairos, or so it seems. And to rush kairos back into chronos is tempting but disastrous. You cannot rush the grieving process that demands kairos, any more than you can rush summer into fall or winter into spring. Spring is promised even as one shovels winter's twelve-inch autograph. But all the shoveling and complaining cannot push one bud of spring onto the old oak tree.

But even as kairos forbids chronos from invading her time zone, one must step into the real world of chronos for certain things that must be done. So, upon arriving home, spending some time in Forest's empty room, letting the night of grief wring water from souls that had cried too much, we made plans to let our daughters know their brother had gone.

Becky had to attend classes at the university, and Rachel had needed to be among her friends back in Hickory, so neither was with us when Forest took his leave. Children, especially teenagers, need their peers around them in times of grief. To expect or require them to be always with the family is a mistake. While they are part of the family, they have friends who constitute an expanded family for them. They need their own kind around them as well as their kin. Already they have formed common denominators of understanding to which the family is not always privy. And these special relationships are vital in times of crisis and stress.

I called Becky in Chapel Hill to tell her the news she had expected and to let her know that Cliff and Lib Price, close friends during and after our Durham days, would pick her up and drive her to Hickory. We cried for a long time over the phone. I tried to offer words of encouragement but could say little that was comforting because I, too, was deep in the valley with her. "Dad," she said, "I don't know how, but some way we will make it. I'll be there as soon as I can. I need you and Mom and Rachel," and her voice trailed off to a soft whisper.

We called the family where Rachel was staying and asked them to bring her home. Taking the phone, Rachel asked, "Dad, is it over?" I told her that it was. "What time?" she asked. When I told her 1:05 A.M., she simply hung up the phone and was home within minutes. She ran into the room and collapsed in our arms. For what seemed like an eternity, she wept torrents, her body shaking with each sob.

And when Becky arrived some hours later, all four of us had a soul-wrenching experience in the privacy of my downstairs study. Someone, hearing our cries, slipped into the room to offer support, but I wanted to have this time together alone. After all, this was the first time we had allowed ourselves to let out our pain in such openness with each other.

There comes a time, I believe, when just the family—the immediate family—needs time alone to ventilate the hurt that has built up during the loved one's dying. This is especially true when the process of dying has been long and drawn out.

We had already planned Forest's funeral service on Friday, September 8, when we knew for sure he could not last much longer.

We decided to request that in lieu of flowers memorial gifts be given to the just-established Robert Forest Smith III Scholarship Fund at Wake Forest University. The service, we determined, would be a celebration of life and an affirmation of faith, and it would be positive and personal.

In my first church after I graduated from seminary, I conducted a funeral service for the mother of one of our deacons. My approach was rather liturgical and somewhat formal, in keeping with my early perceptions about handling death. After the service I visited the home of my deacon. He pulled me aside and said, "Pastor, I appreciate your doing mother's funeral, but there's one thing I wish," and he paused. "I wish you had mentioned *her name* just once." From that point on, every time I did a funeral the phrase of that deacon, who stunned his young pastor, became a principle of preparation to meet the needs of suffering and grieving families. I determined I would make all funeral services personal.

We selected four ministers to lead the service, then selected *our* favorite hymns. After all, the funeral service is for the living, not the dead. Hymns that move the family should be chosen, we felt. Faye's favorite hymn was chosen to be sung first, "God of Our Fathers," followed by my favorite, "God of Grace and God of Glory." We would end with "Lead On, O King Eternal."

Our family determined that we should provide opportunity for the community to express its sympathy and grief by having a special time to receive the people. Too often, we had discovered, the family of a deceased person would give no opportunity for the community to mobilize its grief. Neighbors experience grief when good friends die. They should have some means of dealing with their hurt. No better way, we figured, than a receiving line at the funeral home the night before the service.

As our many friends came by, we discovered that their pain was, in many ways and cases, as raw as ours. But as we mingled our tears, the balm of healing was beginning its work for us all.

Chapter Five

Thursday, September 14, 1978, dawned a beautiful, fall-is-coming day. At two o'clock, we approached the sanctuary of Hickory's First Baptist Church. The 1,350-seat temple of worship was packed and overflowing. High school students were granted leave for the afternoon and created a standing-room-only situation.

Waiting for us in the foyer near the chancel area, the ministers formed a line. Each was fighting back tears. I wondered what would happen in the service. I turned and said, "Boys, give it your best. That will be enough. And thanks."

For years I had entered and preached in that room. But this entrance was different. Always Forest, along with the family, was there. Since he was a little boy, he would come by my office just before the service. We'd visit for a few minutes, he'd give me a hug, and say, "I'll pray for you." Later, when high-fives became popular, he'd high-five me, then slip quickly to join the family in the pastor's pew. He was the most sensitive little boy (and teenager) I have ever known.

To this day I carry in my billfold a note he wrote and put on my desk as I was facing a difficult task—resigning as pastor of the Durham church to go to Hickory.

> Dad,
> I know it's going to be hard but I'll be praying like everything.
> Your Only Son, Forest.
> P.S. God is with you. I love you.

He was eleven years old.

Forest was in the sanctuary today, but not in the pastor's pew. In the solid red oak casket, draped with roses, rested our son. No visit in my office; no hug; no note. Just silence, broken only by the pipe organ's breathing of great hymns and the soft sobbing of a community of faith searching for answers and hoping for some relief and release.

We had asked Mac McGee to read Scripture and offer prayer. He selected, among other passages, the eighth chapter of Romans. When he came to verse 28 he read: "For we know God works all things together for good . . ." He paused, looked up from the text, and confessed with integrity of faith, "We don't know *how*, but we believe he can and will."

As Mac's confession settled on the congregation, I recalled that in the passage Paul did not say, "God works all things together for the *best*," or "for the *better*," but "for *good*." I think that's a fair description of what life's about, even if Paul may not have had in mind my free interpretation. Sometimes we must settle for the *good* because the *better* or *best* is unavailable, given irrevocable circumstances.

Eighteen years later I can say that good things have happened in my life, some of which I share in later chapters. But from my human perspective at that moment, things would have been better, even best, had this tragedy not happened in our lives.

I don't believe everything happens for the best, but I do believe God does his best to bring good out of tragedy if we give him half a chance, if we allow God's power and leadership to reign in our lives. There are times when we feel that the best and the better are gone. The temptation to give up, to chuck the whole pursuit, looms large. But out there somewhere roams the good, just waiting for us to identify, embrace, and implement it in our lives.

But fresh grief is not a suitable environment for discovering God's good gifts or plans. Often, mired in the muck of tragedy, people look for the good too quickly and, not finding it, conclude that God's not going to do anything. Just as we cannot judge a play in the middle of the drama, we cannot judge life in the midst of tragedy. Paul says, "God works all things," but he gives no time frame. He doesn't say "immediately" or "next week." He simply says that "God works." And here's where faith and trust in the goodness of God must focus and rest.

We had asked Larry Phillips to deal with the topic, "Forest as We

Experienced Him." In the course of his presentation, he mentioned that Forest felt strong enough to be gentle. The phrase churned memory of a conversation we had when Forest was eight years old.

"Dad," he said, as I walked by his room. "Would you come in a minute? Got something to tell you."

I settled on the foot of his bed and picked up a loose football trying to escape down the crack between his bed and wall. He was stretched out on the bed with hands interlaced behind his head. We were comfortable.

"Dad, this guy at school is giving me a hard time again."

"The same one?" I asked, remembering other conversations about him.

"Yeah, the same guy. He shoves me every time he gets a chance. I'm getting tired of it."

We talked on a bit. I said little that was definite, trying to stimulate his thinking and not giving any answers. (Maybe I didn't have any.)

"Today he really made me mad. Called me names and hit me on the back—real hard—just as I walked through the door into a classroom."

I didn't say anything. Actually, I was becoming a bit angry because he had not stood up for himself. He stopped talking. Dead silence.

Then he challenged, "What are you going to do about it?"

"What am *I* going to do about it? It's your problem."

"You mean you're not going to help me out? You're not going to do anything?"

Maybe I was tired. The day had been long. I don't know. But I was getting upset with him. *Why doesn't he assert himself?* I thought. *He needs to be more aggressive.*

"No, it's your problem," I said firmly. "I'll help you look at the things you can do, but the final decision is yours. You'll have to decide what you're going to do—how you're going to handle it."

"What *can* I do?" he wanted to know.

My anger surfaced. "You've got two choices. You can stand up and fight him or lie down and let him walk over you!"

Then his anger appeared. "That's the way *you* would do it," he said, his eyes flashing. "You'd fight, wouldn't you?"

I didn't answer.

"Go on, tell me. You'd fight, wouldn't you?"

I calmed down a bit. "I told you I'd help you look at the ways you could handle this. That's all I'm going to do. I'll say it again. You've got two choices: fight or flight."

"No," he said, his anger very visible now. "There's a third way. I can make him my *friend*. You would never have thought of that." His anger flashed, and he dashed out the door.

I sat there a long time. Fight . . . flight . . . friend.

But before Forest could make him a friend, it appeared that a fight was necessary. I made a pass by the house about 4:30 one fall afternoon, and Faye handed me a note from Forest.

"Mom and Dad. I have gone to the park to fight. Don't worry, Rachel is with me. Forest."

I looked at Faye, who stared back at me. "What does this mean?" I asked, looking to his mother, whose every gene he had inherited. I was saying in unspoken language, *He's your son; you ought to know what's going on by instinct.*

She simply said, "We'd better go to the park and see about those children."

We lived in the Duke Park area of Durham. Our house, like many of the old rambling houses of another era in the South, overlooked a lovely park. I didn't know in what area of the park the proposed duel was to take place or who the opponent was. I guessed it was the guy Forest had vowed to make a friend.

I sprinted out the back door, downed the steps three at a time with Faye close behind, and ran around the outer edges of the park until we came to the gated entrance, not seventy-five yards from our door.

And there I saw a most beautiful, cartoonlike scene. Forest had climbed onto the large pillar supporting the wrought-iron arch that spanned the paved entrance to the park. On the other pillar stood six-year-old Rachel. Between the two girded-for-battle children walked Tipper, their 110-pound German shepherd, patrolling the immediate area and constantly glancing up at his charges, wondering what was going on. As simply and seriously as possible, given the authentic Tom Sawyer scenario, I said, "I got your note. What's happening?"

"Well," Forest said, starting his descent down the pillar, "I don't really know. That guy I told you about didn't want to be friends; he wanted to fight. So I told him to meet me at the park here after school, about 3:30. We've been waiting, but he hasn't come."

"Yeah," Rachel said, motioning for me to get her down from her sentinel perch. "He's a scaredy cat," and with that she jumped into my waiting arms and gave me a hug.

"Hey," I said. "Maybe he passed by and saw your army and kept going," I half-teased. "You've got a pretty scary thing going here," I observed. "You, Rachel, and Tipper. That'd be enough to scare me off," and with that the Smith brigade folded their tents of battle and slipped silently, and gratefully, home.

Forest never told me how he approached the "enemy" the next day at school, but in a few days he had exercised the third option and made him a friend.

Randall Lolley brought me back to the present as he cleared his throat and looked at us with reddened eyes. We had asked him to read excerpts from Forest's essay in his Wake Forest application. That part of the service we had labeled "Forest as He Experienced Himself."

"The last sentence of Forest's essay looms largest," Randall said. "After describing himself, his life, his dreams, his hopes for the future, and his close and appreciated relationship with his family, he wrote: 'I would change nothing.'

"This sentence," Randall observed, "contains his last written words. We sense that while his life was short, it was deep. While he would change nothing in terms of his relationship with his family that was so deep and satisfying, I daresay one cannot read this essay without predicting that had he lived he would have changed much that is wrong with our world."

Dr. W. Perry Crouch, seasoned person and pastor, walked slowly and deliberately to the large pulpit. Gripping both sides of the pulpit desk, and looking with misty eyes at the large gathering, he puckered his mouth, seeking composure that did not come immediately.

Expectantly the congregation looked up to this servant of God as he readied himself to deal with his assigned topic: "God as We Experience Him in Tragedy," no doubt something everyone present was wondering about. Finally, he spoke, calling the essay written by Forest "one of the modern miracles of our day; honest and sincere, written by one so young." Then he called attention to faith, observing that "a lot of times we do not really pay much attention to what we believe. We just live from day to day. And then something happens—some tragedy maybe, some shocking event—and suddenly we are brought face to face with eternal verities that we can't dodge. Then we stop to ask, 'What about that? What do we believe?'

"For just a few moments," he invited, "let's think about what God is like. What do you think God is like? Well, we are used to saying that God is all-powerful. God is truth and righteousness and all of that. But greater than all of these we are told that God is love.

"One day a young person said to me, 'Let me tell you something that I heard your son Bob say the other day.' The young man told me that a group of boys were talking about what they would do if an accident happened to them, especially since all of them had just gotten their driver's licenses. They asked Bob what he would do. He said, 'Why, if I was to have an accident, I would call my daddy immediately.' One of them said, 'Your daddy?' 'Yes. And my daddy would ask, when I told him I'd had an accident, 'Are you hurt?' And then if I said I'm not hurt, he would say, 'Stay right there and I'll be there as soon as I can.'

"I didn't think too much of that then," Dr. Crouch admitted. "But a few years later when that same son, then a forty-two-year-old surgeon, developed a terminal disease, and we knew we were going to lose him, I remembered that day and went to my knees and said, 'If he could believe that about his father, an earthly father with faults and failures, can't I believe it about my Heavenly Father?'"

With deep emotion gripping his body and voice, Perry said, "So Romans 8:28 came to have new meaning. *God works in all things for good to those who love the Lord.* He doesn't cause accidents that bring death. He's not responsible for our actions because, you see, he made us—the crown of all his creation—persons who could think and make our own decisions.

"Then he challenged us to think and to live and to make our decisions. He never promised he would protect us from every physical harm or every disease or every accident. We are in a world where all of these things are present. And he warned us that the world is real; that there would be troubles and heartaches and difficulties and accidents.

"He can't protect us from all these adversities and make us free at the same time," he said, and paused, giving time for the truth to settle into the minds of his listeners.

"I remember some years ago," Perry said, "that a mother in our town had a six-year-old daughter who was beginning school. She said, 'Oh, I can't possibly trust my little girl to walk the few blocks to the school building. She might get run over. She might get hurt. I can't do it.'

"So she took her every day in her car and then parked her car right outside the window of the classroom, and said to her daughter, 'I'll be sitting in the car just outside.' But that little girl didn't adjust in the schoolroom. She was restless. She wanted to go to the window and see her mother sitting outside. Somehow the arrangement didn't become the security the mother thought it would be.

"God didn't make that mistake with us. He created us so we could make our decisions and learn from our experiences in life itself. But he did say if you choose me and want me as your Heavenly Father, I will never leave you or forsake you.

"We've got a wonderful example here in Forest because we've got a person who lived so much and came to feel so much in such a short time. And now he has moved on to be with his Lord, with eternal life before him.

"And yet, what we need most of all in these moments is the realization that we know a God of love whose love is broad enough and deep enough and wide enough to include us. And when we need him, we can call on him in any trouble or difficulty, at any moment, day or night, and he will not forsake us. In time, we will learn from this tragedy that God will never leave us alone. Indeed, God works in all things for good to those who love him and to those who are called according to his purpose."

Later, my father, who was crushed by the death of the grandson bearing his own name, commented, "Perry's talk helped me so much as I tried to understand where God is in all this." I, too, was helped, but at that precise moment I was on an emotional and theological roller coaster. The highs came, but so did the lows. A high, given birth by Perry, would rise nobly as the congregation stood to sing "Lead On, O King Eternal." Emotions were unashamedly wetting faces, as men and women, boys and girls, struggled to sing the great words that reminded us "the day of march has come."

As we sang, I knew the evening of death, the kairos that had enveloped us for the past days, would now struggle to march us back into the chronos.

Following the benediction, the organist blew the dust out of the pipes as he played "Lead On, O King Eternal" for the postlude. We walked down the long aisle of pews, facing friends and neighbors, and saw their tears that became support as the strains of the great old hymn rose, recalling for us that "henceforth in fields of conquest, Thy tents shall be our home."

As we arrived in the narthex of the church, the last stanza of the hymn came to me in total recall:

Lead on, O King Eternal, We follow, not with fears;
For gladness breaks like morning, Where'er Thy face appears;
Thy cross is lifted o'er us, We journey in its light:
The crown awaits the conquest; Lead on, O God of might.

I stood there for a moment, looked back to the chancel and Forest's lonely wooden box, and wondered: *Will gladness ever break like morning? Can I still follow my King without fear?* Even then the anger began to heat up again.

In seconds I half-smiled to myself: *This is what preaching and worship are all about: inspiration, stimulation, then before clearing the narthex, the old feelings grab again, pushing the just-inspired worshiper back into his cave, not unlike Elijah plunging from Mount Carmel's high moment to the wilderness where he almost starved to death. The angel came for Elijah. And fed him. Would he come for me? Would he feed my starving soul?* But just then the funeral director interrupted my thoughts. "We must get you in the cars fast," he urged. "If you start talking with this crowd, we'll never get to the cemetery."

When the long procession of cars was finally in place, we began the fifteen-mile trek to the burying ground of my ancestors where generations of Smiths and Benfields are buried in large numbers. We pulled into the modest cemetery that sits on a high hill. My forebears had founded the little church and built their first building there.

At the graveside service we were reminded that "the ground on which we now stand will become sacred to this hurting family in the days and years ahead because it holds locked within its grip the body of a son they loved so deeply." Chronos was struggling to exert itself, as thoughts about beautiful flowers, a gravestone to be designed, and family members who needed to get back home to the daily run of duty came dimly into focus.

That night family and friends gathered in our home as we reviewed the events of the day. Finally, someone urged me to lie down. "You're exhausted," she observed with accuracy. The couch was quickly vacated and other seats sought. I lay down with a pillow under my head and rested.

Immediately voices lowered in respect for my rest. "No," I said. "Please keep talking. I won't talk, but I want to hear you. I need for you to talk." And they did. At that very tired moment, what they said was not as important as that they were there to say it. There is something soothing and comforting about the sound of friends talking. The sounds of voices bring hard evidence that people are surrounding you with love as they move to subjects that remind you life *does* go on, and that they will be there for you as you pick up the pieces life has scattered around you.

As the evening of death merges into the night of grief, you learn that neither of these time periods provides appropriate occasions for making long-term plans. During these emotional days of grief, only immediate and routine details should be dealt with. Unless you are pressured to make major decisions, don't! Sometimes people make life-changing decisions that are better placed on hold until life returns to a more normal pace. In an effort to deal with grief, some people decide to sell the home place to escape memories encased in old surroundings. Such major decisions should be delayed several months if at all possible. The evening of death and the night of grief are wildernesses in which a person should have only one goal: *to work through them.*

Friends may offer beach houses or mountain cottages immediately after a funeral, urging grieving persons "to get away from all this for a spell. You'll be better when you return." The kindness is notable. But to seize upon their offer may be the worst mistake you can make. At some point you will have to reenter the reality of the empty chair and empty bed. The sooner the better. The longer reentry is delayed, the longer the night of grief. Take a rain check, assuring benevolent friends you will take them up on their offer in six months.

The transition period between the evening of death and the night of grief is a time to let the soul hang out. It is a time of hurting, and the hurt should be allowed to play out its role in the grief process. To short-circuit the process is to delay the process, and delayed grief is difficult to deal with.

Often families are judged by how well they are "holding up," signified by smiles, an upbeat facade, little or no weeping, the pretense that nothing has happened. Some well-meaning but ill-advised souls think that acting as an ambassador from sunshine land is a badge of the mourner's faith. But such "holding up" is nothing more than holding back natural and normal human emotions that must be allowed expression.

I'm often asked how Mrs. Widow is doing following her husband's recent death. If she is processing her grief properly, my answer shocks some people: "Doing absolutely great. She cries and laughs, and cries and laughs, and cries and laughs." Some people do not understand that tears make sense in times of grief. To paraphrase Scripture: "Do not quench the spirit of hurt that is crying for expression."

Hurt is a reality and will find some avenue for expression. You can allow the proper expression, or you can squash it, but it will eventually squeeze itself out in all sorts of inappropriate actions.

The evening of death passes, but the night of grief comes—whether one is prepared or not. And in that night of nights, which is both moonless and starless, you search for the candlelight of faith to lead you. And you pray that you will find it somehow, somewhere.

PART 2

The Night of Grief

Chapter Six

The exit of the evening of death is fairly well defined—the funeral is over, friends return home, belongings are repositioned, and a feeling of lostness bores deep into mind, body, and soul. You know the days ahead will not be easy; you feel night tightening its garment around you, but there's no warmth. Coldness permeates your very being, making normal actions difficult, like muscles cramping, refusing to follow the mind.

Ezekiel skipped from the evening of death to the morning of duty with no indication of what happened in his night of grief. God had intimated to him that he would have a night of grief but directed him to "sigh, but not aloud." One feels for Ezekiel, knowing that tears shed inside the soul are hotter and more searing than tears that flow properly on the face.

Too often there's the temptation to wrap oneself in the cloak of inactivity, refusing to face the return to calendar responsibilities where routines of reality are required and are no longer graced by understanding associates and friends.

Just how quickly chronos would extend its scepter of power became clear when I suddenly realized that my weekly newspaper column was due three days after Forest's funeral. For two years I had written a column for several area newspapers titled "Looking Homeward," a perspective on family life. Charles Deal, editor of the *Hickory News*, a unique and widely read weekly, had suggested over a cup of coffee that I consider such an endeavor. The column's immediate acceptance stimulated expansion into other newspapers in the Piedmont area of North Carolina.

"Charles," I said over the phone. "I know the deadline's today and . . ." But before I could finish my sentence, Charles said, "Hey, forget it. We'll cover for you. You've been through too much to think of writing anything. No problem," he said. "We'll handle it for you."

"No," I told him. "I need to write. I will write. Just give me until this afternoon."

"Okay," he said. "But you don't have to do this, you know." But I knew I did. Writing had always been therapeutic for me; it was not only a challenge but a tool for mobilizing whatever frustration tried to imprison me.

Most people have some activity that's a source of healing, something that provides an outlet but also becomes an inlet for new resources, new perspectives, and fresh strength. As I struggled with the transition from *evening of death* to *night of grieving*, I needed access to all available tools for coping. And I knew that writing would at least help.

On the way downstairs to my study, I had to pass Forest's room. His room occupied one end of the lower level and my study and library the other. Between our territories was a large den with a fireplace, where he and I often met on neutral ground for conversation as logs burned hypnotically, enriching the companionship between father and son.

I paused briefly at the door of his room, then entered and sat on the edge of his bed. Sobs racked my body. Quickly I left and walked past the fireplace. Its smell of wood burnings brought memories too painful to recall but not too deep for words I knew I had to write.

And the words came, along with tears that drenched the old Smith-Corona, blurring vision. I needed to talk with Forest. Such a need is natural in the early days following one's loss. The loved one is still too present to be dismissed from life's daily realities. Some people report actually feeling the lost one's presence so vividly they can actually see the person and hear the loved one's voice. Many people are awakened in the night by a sense of the person's presence and even audible words. The mind can play tricks on us, but at the same time it may be opening new areas of communication that seem unusual and perhaps even unnatural.

One man told his pastor that he constantly felt his wife's presence and heard her voice. "What shall I do?" he asked. The pastor properly blessed the experience and encouraged him to talk to his wife as best as he could. I'm sure various disciplines of psychology could offer explanations for such phenomenal experiences, reminding us that perception is reality but not always real. And I understand that stance. But when the night of grief casts all sorts of shadows, a person responds to the shadows until the process of grief allows an uplifting of the face. Then one can see the sun and recognize shadows as shadows. But until that time comes, a person must deal with what light is possible.

So I wrote my article in the form of a letter to my son. In the letter (reprinted in Appendix 1) I told him how much I missed him, and I reviewed for him (but mostly for me) the accident and something of the pain we were feeling. I related that we were wandering in the wordless silence of questioning spirits, trying to make sense of it all. I told him that we were seeing many people's lives changed through his death. But in all honesty, I confessed, our one desire was to have him back the way he was. In his life he touched hundreds of people, but in his death he was touching many more.

Frankly, there is little comfort, especially in the early night of grief, in being told that the death of your loved one is having a wonderful and positive impact on other persons. You are grateful but deeply ambivalent; your gratitude is laced with almost a resentment that people are experiencing an uplift in their lives while your loved one enjoys no such blessing. In time, you get beyond these feelings, but not in the dark hours of grief's night.

I confessed that we were still asking Why? Why did this happen? Why did it happen to him? Contrary to much theology, asking why is not irreligious and does not signify a lack of faith. Asking why is as natural as breathing when something happens that's not supposed to happen, or when some incident disrupts your life, or when your dreams fall about your feet like shattered glass.

When you reach the no-man's land of life, and there's no road map, the question Why? fills the soul as surely as frustration fills the mind. When no logical answers are found, the Why? resounds as an echo from the deep tunnel that has no light at its other end.

Although we may never find an answer, there is some measure of healing happening even in the asking. At least we get our question on the table, out where we can admit it and see it and deal with it. There is an honesty in asking why, even in asking "Why, God?" Jesus did it. "My God, why have you forsaken me?" There was integrity in Jesus' confession to God of his pain and confusion.

I hand-delivered the column to Charles Deal at his downtown office. "Charlie," I said. "You may need to edit this severely. It is mighty emotional, maybe too much so for general consumption. If you don't run it at all, I'll understand."

I left and later received a phone call from Charles's office. "Mr. Deal said to be sure to mail your column to the other newspapers. He thinks they will run it as we're going to do." Two of the newspapers not only ran the article but made it the lead front-page story. Editors across North Carolina picked it up and ran it as a feature; some columnists used it in editorials. Over the next weeks and months it was reproduced by a dozen newspapers.

I found one newspaper's lead-in to the article interesting and revealing. The headline covered eight columns in bold type: "Minister Looks at Son's Death and Asks 'Why?'" Whatever thoughts motivated the headline writer, his choice of words expressed what is all too common in the minds of the so-called laity: *Ministers are not human!* They do not have the same emotions, feelings, thoughts, and perspectives as the rest of humanity. That a minister has questions, that he or she would dare ask "Why?" is headline news.

Of course, workers in other professions face similar temptations *not to be human.* Physicians, for instance, seldom subject themselves to the annual physical examinations they require of others.

I recall meeting a young doctor, a good friend and church member, in the hospital hallway while his wife was in the labor room struggling to give birth to their first child.

"What are you doing?" I asked, as I watched him juggle charts in frustration.

"Making rounds," he said.

"I thought your wife was in labor."

"She is, but I thought I'd just get on with business."

I didn't respond to his attempt to deny his humanity, but in a short while he came by the chaplain's office where I had stopped for coffee and a chat. "I just can't concentrate on my patients right now," he said, moving to the coffee urn.

"Jack," I said. "Why don't you just be what you are right now?"

"What's that?" he asked.

"A nervous husband like all the rest of us when our wives are having babies. Just be human for the next few hours. You cannot be a doctor until that baby is born," I declared, and I hugged him like a brother.

In the evening of death and the night of grieving, titles and professional status are stripped from us, and we all stand on level ground. There are no professionals in the wildernesses of life, whatever our training and lifestyle; we are amateurs all. We struggle as best we can. And when we refuse our amateur status, intent on maintaining our professional role, the results are often disastrous.

When my eighty-five-year-old father died, some eight years after Forest's death, I learned what not taking time to grieve could do. Dad lived alone following my mother's death. He was active, always on the go, so neighbors did not think it strange they had not seen him in several days. Finally, two neighbors decided to check on him. He had been dead two days, comfortably reclining in his favorite chair in the den.

Over the years I have urged families to view their loved ones after death. There's something healing about saying a final good-bye. Viewing the loved one's body brings the reality of death into focus, a fact that must be faced if grief is to be properly processed. Often people say, "I don't want to see the body. I want to remember her the way she was." That's understandable, but "the way she was" is *dead*. Death is a part of the life experience, the final part, and must be dealt with as final. Saying goodbye is the first step in turning the loved one loose—a *must* in the process of grief that leads to healing.

I wanted desperately to see my father one last time, though the hot weather, I was told, had hurriedly done its damage. The funeral director urged me not to view his body. Since he pulled no punches in graphically describing the condition of my father's body, I sensed he was seeing me as a minister, not as a son who had just lost his father. He most likely would not have been so frank with the "average" grieving family.

The temptation to minister to people in terms of their roles is often overwhelming. But one's role is of little value when one is struggling with emotions created by illness or loss, and refusal to shed the role is detrimental. Just as counterproductive is the inability of friends and other professionals to see the person in his or her human-ness. A physician in a hospital bed is no longer a doctor. He is a patient, just as scared of surgery as the next person (maybe even more so because he knows how many things can go wrong). A counselor standing at the casket of his loved one is as vulnerable and helpless as any counselee he's ever helped.

Both Dad and Mom had requested that I conduct their funeral services. So I took charge of Dad's funeral arrangements and delivered the meditation. Following the funeral, the details of closing the home place and processing legal documents occupied my time. And upon returning home, I conducted five funerals in almost as many days.

A few months later depression set in. I was walking around and functioning, but I was depressed nonetheless.

I visited a chaplain friend at the hospital. At the end of the session he said, "You know what's going on, don't you?"

"Yeah," I said. "Delayed grief. I haven't taken time to deal with Dad's death. I've been too busy doing my thing."

"Something else," he said. "You never had opportunity to tell your dad goodbye."

"I couldn't, you know. The body was in too bad a shape, they told me."

As I turned for the door, he said, "You've got to get a new picture of your dad, not the one you have now of a partially decomposed body." I nodded and headed home.

Several nights later I had a dream. Dad was on a ladder, as I had seen him many times when he had climbed to the roof to do some repair work. He was about forty-five, in the prime of his life. His muscular and suntanned arms reflected healthy sweat, and his hat was perched at its usual jaunty angle.

Dad spoke: "Son, I'm okay. I'm okay. Don't worry," and I jerked awake as a feeling of relief bathed my mind, body, and soul.

I called the chaplain first thing the next morning and told him my dream. "Thank God," he said. "The Holy Spirit does work through our dreams." The depression that had tormented and was on the verge of imprisoning me ceased almost immediately.

Depression has many causes. Unresolved anger turned on one-self can generate depression. The chief culprit in my case was anger at being unable to bid my father a proper farewell. But some of the anger I felt when Forest died was stimulated by off-hand, insensi-tive comments made by well-meaning people who had come to offer support in our evening of death.

Several friends were sitting at the breakfast table in our home the day before the funeral service. I came in for a cup of coffee. As I poured sugar and cream into the black stuff that had embalmed me during the evening of death, one of the women said, "You know, this is bad, losing Forest and all that. But just think: he will never have to go through all the things the rest of us will." She paused, but no one said anything. She continued: "He'll never have to take college tests. I think it's fortunate this happened before he had to go to Wake Forest and take all those horrible college exams like my sons did."

I must have mumbled something in response. But what I wanted to do was yell at her! To tell her she didn't know the first thing from squat about what she was saying. She was not intentionally being mean or unkind; she was not that kind of person. She simply felt she must say something, even if it was wrong. And it was! As I reflect upon my friend's words, and the motivation behind them, I think she was trying to say that Forest was better off in heaven, something we all believed, but there were much better ways to convey that concept.

My friend was in the great tradition of Job's comforters. They, too, felt they had to say something, even though they really had nothing to say. They thought, no doubt, that by doing much talking they could somehow ease the pain of Job's loss.

Job's friends also took the occasion of his pain to discuss theology. And I met that attempt out in the yard where a group of friends and relatives had gathered when the house would hold no more.

"I guess you heard about my wreck three months ago," said a healthy-looking man.

"Yes," I said. "That must have been terrible."

"Oh, it was. Let me tell you something," he said. "I wouldn't be standing here today if God had not been with me."

Again, I must have mumbled something, though I can't remember what. But my unspoken thoughts were in an uproar. *Was God not with Forest? Did he forsake him? Why would he be with you and not with my son? Where was God when Forest couldn't avoid that pier?*

I wondered what would happen if I voiced these thoughts to my friend, who had no idea what he had said. He is not a mean person; quite the contrary. He is a loving and kind person and would have been deeply hurt had he realized the implications of his statements.

That God was with him and with my son is a faith reality I readily embrace—now, and before Forest's accident. But at that moment, in my wilderness process of finding some place to stand and survive, to imply that God was present with one person and absent from another was not at all helpful.

Tragedy is not the time to discuss theology, to confront, or to correct; it is a time for comfort. Yet somehow we think we must explain what happened in terms of theology, making sure God is protected. We try to discover reasons for the tragedy, as if knowledge of the tragedy will somehow lessen the pain.

I gained one significant insight through this experience: *knowledge does not relieve hurt.* One can accidentally break a leg. The doctor can explain exactly what is wrong with the leg. In great detail, he can catalogue, complete with radiological evidence, what's going on in the broken limb. He may ask, "Do you understand this?" The patient nods Yes. The doctor leaves after infusing the patient with knowledge, but the pain does not leave with him. With all the knowledge, the leg still hurts.

Knowledge does have power; it *is* power, at least in some quarters and circumstances. But it is powerless to comfort, just as it is powerless to heal. At best, knowledge can give us facts; it cannot give us faith, nor can it right the wrong or ease the pain. The pain remains far beyond the funeral service, and long after the crowd has gone.

Most of us know what to do immediately when death comes into the lives of friends. We call by phone and in person, often taking food. But after food and funeral, what then? Here's where most of us run out of road map. The common complaint I hear from people grieving over loss is this: "My friends just seem to ignore my tragedy, never mentioning it or giving me a chance to talk about it." One mother who had lost her son told me, "When I went back to work, the people smiled and were friendly, but they never spoke about my son. They didn't say anything. It was business as usual, as if nothing had ever happened to me." With tears she told me, "They simply tiptoe around my tragedy, and that makes me angry. And it hurts."

Most people assume that grieving persons do not want to be reminded of their loss. *That is not true!* They want to talk about their loved ones, and they simply need someone to listen with sensitivity. There's no such thing as "business as usual" when one has lost a loved one. The loss is real, and the losing person wants comforters who are real in their approach.

I was so grateful to those friends who would let me talk about Forest. Harold Rose, a man I met some months later as I traveled through the night of grief, was one of the most helpful persons who came into my life. Harold was not a trained counselor but rather a successful businessman and father of three. He never knew Forest, but he would drop by my office two or three times a week for a "free cup of coffee," he'd say, trying to hide his real reason. When we had settled into comfortable chairs, with hot cups of coffee warming our hands, Harold would say, "Now, tell me about Forest," and I was off and running.

Harold never tried to close a conversation; that was my job, he figured. When I'd slow down my recitation about Forest, he instinctively asked strategic questions that kept me talking. He never tried to dry my tears but often cried with me. Somehow this sensitive man knew that crying does not hurt, that it releases hurt and ultimately brings healing. He never tried to change the subject; he just let me talk until I ran down.

Less than three years after Harold came into my life, I conducted his funeral, one of the hardest in my ministry. Was it fantasy or faith that caused me to wonder: *Is this why Harold wanted to know so much about Forest? Did he somehow know he'd see him before I would?*

In the early months following Forest's death, I appreciated many other people who would say by pen or phone: "Just want you to know I'm thinking of you." Or, "You are daily in my prayers." Some said, "I'm hurting with you." And when they said that in person, they gave me opportunity to reveal what was going on with me at that moment.

During the evening of death, and on into the night of grief, some mis-thinking persons would say, "I know just how you feel." They didn't, not unless they had lost a child! I'm sure I had said, in times past when a person had lost a mate, "I know how you feel." But I didn't, and I never said it again. I learned that a better, more honest response is "I don't know how you feel, not really, but it must be terrible." Such a statement opens all sorts of doors through which one can walk with another.

Not many weeks after Forest's death, a fellow minister in Raleigh, North Carolina, lost his son in a terrible automobile accident. Though the minister and I hardly knew each other, I was moved to call him on the phone. With his Scottish accent he asked, "Do you ever get over this hurt?" I told him I didn't really know, but I doubted it. Maybe, I told him, it's like losing one of your legs in an accident. For weeks you suffer, totally incapacitated. But slowly healing happens. Crutches bridge the gap, and shoulders of friends support, easing the pain of learning to walk again. Soon, I suggested, an artificial leg is fitted. With proper therapy you learn to walk again, taking up the daily run of duty with much the same routine as before. Except for the limp.

But you never forget that at one time in your life you had two good legs. The limp won't let you forget. Nothing can make you forget. You function much as before. Outwardly most people never know you are missing a leg. After awhile even your close friends forget you lost a leg. Except for the limp.

But you never forget that at one time you had a son. You function again. You live and laugh and love again. In time, most people may not know or remember. Except for the limp.

Chapter Seven

My night of grief was deep and real, but the morning of duty started flashing signals of responsibility that flickered like early stars in heaven's canopy of darkness. No doubt about it—Ezekiel had his night of grief. But maybe, just maybe, his night of grief and his morning of duty were so interwoven that he could not draw a line between the two.

Perhaps his morning of duty and night of grief were one and the same. The perception gained credibility as I struggled in my night of grief, wondering how I would ever get to the morning of duty. I could not draw a definite line separating the two because I kept alternating between them.

But just as I believe there is life after death for our loved ones, I also believe there is life for us after their death. And we must seek that life as soon as reasonably possible. There are times when you really wonder, even doubt, that you will ever live again. You simply go through the motions of living, more an existence than a life. What once seemed so important no longer has meaning. Life becomes as tasteless and bland as the food you once attacked with delight. What was once beauty becomes drab, and what once excited now depresses.

At night sleep denies its presence, and when it finally comes, it brings little rest or comfort. In the mornings you cry more. Sleep has deadened senses for a spell, but awakeness crashes upon you. You are vulnerable, and life tends to cave in. You fight for control.

That's why it is so important to assume routines and duty as soon as possible without overindulging as a means of escape. A healthy balance between work and not-work, duty and not-duty, is essential.

Reentry is always difficult. When a spacecraft is brought out of orbit and back to earth, there is danger as it reenters earth's atmosphere—the danger that it will burn up as the friction of the fast-moving craft encounters the density of earth's atmosphere. When a person reenters the atmosphere of the "daily run of duty," the density of earthly demands creates friction that can burn up one's life-craft. As with the astronaut, care must be used as one reenters the normal activities and requirements of daily living.

A part of the reentry plan and process is physical exercise. Brisk walking, even jogging if your physical stamina permits, should be a daily assignment for persons dealing with the night of grief. If possible, breaking a sweat is helpful and healthy.

One of my friends was fighting depression over the loss of a loved one. He was advised by his psychiatrist to get off the couch and work in his garden.

"I don't have a garden," argued my friend.

"Do you have a yard?" asked the doctor. "Do you have a shovel? Well, take the shovel and dig a hole. Then fill it up. And keep doing that until you break a sweat," ordered the doctor.

As physical exertion gradually makes its contribution to our well-being, the time arrives for testing the waters of normal responsibilities. When I finally looked seriously at my calendar, I realized that the First Baptist Church of Boone, North Carolina, had scheduled me for a preaching mission the first week in October. The pastor and several of his members visited us many times in our wilderness at Baptist Hospital, offering genuine support. In a phone call, the pastor assured me that the church would not expect me to honor the commitment, given the circumstances. I told him I wanted to keep the appointment. This was something I needed to do and wanted to do.

But I could not anticipate how difficult that first sermon would be. I was in tears long before my time to preach. The hymns crushed me. I learned that for months—even years, even to this day—music has a strange, tear-producing, and emotional effect on me. The poet's declaration that "music has power to soothe the savage breast" was lost on me. I discovered its power to stimulate, not soothe, the savaging feelings of grief. (Perhaps the poet had other matters in mind.)

When time came for my sermon, God's presence provided a soothing effect music could not. I never cease being amazed at how present and powerful God's spirit becomes when needed the most! God's promise to be always with us is a promise we can count on. Our weakness becomes opportunity for his strength.

I knew I had to mention the wilderness I was in. To ignore present reality is never a good way to begin a sermon. I hardly remember any of what I said. I do recall expressing appreciation for their support and asking for their indulgence as we shared together during the week. Many times during my sermons throughout the week, I was emotionally overcome, sometimes wondering if I could finish. I felt as though I were bleeding on the altar, but the congregation's understanding and support pulled me through, an experience I shall never forget.

Each morning that week we had a prayer breakfast. At every service, both morning and evening, I noticed a young man listening intently. On Tuesday morning I made a special effort to meet him.

"I'm Frank Graham," he said.

I looked carefully at his features, feeling I had seen them somewhere before. "Are you Ann Graham Lotz's brother?" I asked. He smiled and said yes.

"I thought you favored her," I observed, recalling that I often described Ann as a female version of her father. "And that makes you Billy Graham's namesake," I guessed. He nodded yes and we sat down for a second cup of coffee. At that time Franklin was going through some wildernesses himself. We shared our separate but not totally different pilgrimages as we both wondered what God had in store for us.

Franklin's genuine sympathy over the loss of my son was moving. I shall never forget the clearness of his eyes as he expressed his concern. "I don't know what in the world I would do if I lost a child," he said, voicing the feelings of all parents. His open and honest confession was good counseling. He made no pretense of complete understanding.

At that time, I didn't know what I would do either. But I soon learned that life had to be reentered. And I was trying. God knows, I was trying. The week with the understanding people at Boone was a step forward in my journey through the night of grief.

My reentry was stepped up by conversations with the pastoral search committee of Fifth Avenue Baptist Church in Huntington, West Virginia, that had begun four weeks before tragedy struck our family.

For the past two years I had served as executive director of Market Ministry, Inc., an experimental effort backed by some two dozen business executives to put into place in industry a value system predicated on Christian ethics. As the two-year experiment approached its final months, we knew the organization would have to expand or close down. At that time I had a growing feeling that God was leading me back into the pastorate and had agreed to talk with the Fifth Avenue committee.

Arrangements were made for the committee to hear me preach in a neighboring city. On that scheduled Sunday morning in October I received an early telephone call from the committee chair informing me the airport in Huntington was fogged in and their chartered flight was grounded. They would not be able to make the eleven o'clock service and would need to reschedule our meeting.

We made the thirty-mile trip to the church in silence, our family's grief now burdened with disappointment. Frustration filled my thoughts. *God*, I said to myself, not willing for the family to hear my anger, *would you please get in your Black Chair?* The anger I felt was not as raw as in the hospital the night Forest died. Maybe I was getting more perspective as I struggled to approach the morning of duty as courageously as Ezekiel. I don't know. Now my approach to God was more civil, much like my children's approach when their frustration made Black Chair time with me necessary.

But when I started "Black Chairing," as our children termed it, the frustration became fear, then pure anger. *God, is this just another divine wild goose chase you tossed into the puzzle of my life? After all, you are in charge of weather. Of all things, fog? Come on, and in October? Why don't you make things a bit simpler? You could use a good business manager, you know?*

Then self-pity, that quagmire of slimy self-defeat, engulfed me almost to my neck. *After all I've been through, and am not through yet, this happens! What are you trying to say to me? Why don't you just up and say it? You spoke directly to your servants in the Old Testament. Why not now? Why not to me?*

My anger at God kept building. *How can I preach with all these feelings flailing about in my soul? You tell me that, God!* For most of the trip I was in such a mood. I can't remember all I felt and said silently to God, but it was a prayer mode I used many times in the months ahead. But now I had to put on my game face. I had to preach.

"What Do You Do with a Wilderness?" was a sermon I had prepared and delivered several years ago. With the night of grief casting dark shadows that blinded creativity, I had retrieved and reworked this sermon that outlined fairly well my basic theology about tragedies and hardships.

There come times in our lives when we must retreat and reconsider what we believed before hardship nailed us to the wall. Both Old and New Testaments are filled with "It is written," reminding us that when negative experiences come into our lives, what was "written"—what was true and real in good times—is still real and true in bad times. Sometimes grasping that reality is difficult, but it is helpful and healing to recall in our valleys what we experienced and believed when on our mountains.

I revisited the sermon now with a more personal interest. Before Forest died I had spoken *about* the wilderness; now I would be speaking *from* the wilderness. The sermon was based on Acts 2:28: "Thou hast made known to me the ways of life." Even in the good times, scattered with a few rather shallow valleys, I had discovered that "the ways of life are the ways of the wilderness."

Even a casual reading of the Bible reveals that God's people spent much of their time in some kind of wilderness. A reading of secular history reminds us that people spend more time in wildernesses than anywhere else. The question comes: "What do you do with a wilderness?" I think we have two choices: "cop out" or "cope with." A wilderness can certainly defeat you, though I doubt you can defeat it. But defeating a wilderness is not necessary. The point—the way to cope with it—is to *go through it.*

In Psalm 23 David shows us what to do with a wilderness: "Though I walk *through* the valley [wilderness] of the shadow of death . . ." (Psalm 23:4a RSV). The psalmist continues: "I will not live there; I will not let it defeat me; it will not hold me; I will go *through it.*"

Most of us agree that a wilderness is something we go through. But *how* do we go through it?

First, we accept the reality of it. There is absolutely no virtue in denying that one is in a wilderness. There's no gain in denying it hurts, that it's painful, or that there's a problem that's creating pressure. There are two things worse than crying in the wilderness: *not crying* in the wilderness, and crying out that you are *not in a wilderness.*

Some years ago I was staying in a hotel in Houston, Texas. One morning the elevator got stuck between the seventeenth and eighteenth floors. Five of us shared the little square room that suddenly became a wilderness. When it dawned upon us that we were not moving, we started reacting. One woman turned white immediately. Another said, "I must sit down. I must, I must." She did. Right on the floor. One man said over and over, totally ignoring our situation, "I'm due at an important meeting. I must go. I must go now." (You wanted to tell him to go on and you'd follow him!) Somebody said, "Don't think we are stuck—it'll move any moment." We all wished she were right.

But the first thing we had to do was to realize that we were stuck and in trouble. We were uncomfortable and scared, and there was danger. In that elevator wilderness, either openly or silently, we admitted we were stuck in a rather cramped wilderness.

Our next action—and this is always the second step—was to discover what resources we had.

What could we do? First, we tried all the buttons—up, down, open door, close door. Nothing worked. Then we noticed a telephone encased in a little box on the wall. I jerked the door open, picked up the phone, and a pleasant voice answered, "May I help you?" I answered, "I surely hope so!" I reported our condition, our location, and our desire to get out as soon as they found it convenient!

In less than five minutes we slowly started moving downward. On the lobby level the door opened. No welcome committee was there. No one. Just people busy about life. Sometimes when you finally make it through a wilderness, most people may never realize what you've been through, not even the people closest to you. Though some wildernesses can be shared, some of the deepest valleys are too personal to be shared except with professional counselors. But sharing with someone is imperative, or the experience may devastate even the strongest among us. In our elevator wilderness someone had helped. We never saw him or her. We don't know what was done, but some person got us out of our wilderness.

When we're in a wilderness, *the second thing we do is to discover and identify our resources.* They may not be as many as we'd like, but often they are more than we realize, and just enough to get us through it. Accepting the reality of our resources is a major step in getting through the wilderness.

And now, the major action, the step of faith beyond ourselves: *Accept the reality of God's power to help.*

Just as someone reached for the phone in the elevator, we must reach through prayer to the power and presence of God. Then we hear that consoling and still, small voice, "I will help you. I will be with you. You are not left alone. I am with you always." And help comes. As in the elevator, the help is often unseen, the way unknown, but from that invisible source, it comes. And it is sufficient.

God does not always come in the way we want, but always in the way we need. As Alex Haley's grandmother put it: "The Lord doesn't always come when we think he ought to, but he's always on time."

The Hebrews, in their wilderness, did not reach for that power. The writer of Hebrews says they wandered forty years in the wilderness because "of their unbelief" (Hebrews 3:19 RSV). They didn't believe God could help them. And God couldn't because they wouldn't let him.

In the wilderness we have to accept our resources *and* our limitations. But in accepting our limitations, we need to remember that God has none, except when limited by our lack of faith.

Imagine: I can limit God! I do it by refusing to believe that God can. The Hebrews limited God, and so can we. And when we limit God, we always end up living in a wilderness.

A wilderness is something you go through by coping with it, not copping out. When you find yourself in any kind of wilderness, admit you're in it, check your resources—your network of support—and reach out to God's power and promise: "I am with you."

There's an old gospel hymn I used to hear as a lad. It may not be great music, but it has a great message.

> When in affliction's valley,
>   I'm treading the road of care,
> My Savior helps me to carry
>   My cross when heavy to bear,
> My feet entangled with briars,
>   Ready to cast me down;
> My Savior whispered His promise,
>   Never to leave me alone.
> No, never alone. No, never alone.
>   He promised never to leave me,
> Never to leave me alone.

After following him for nearly six decades through all sorts of wildernesses, I can report that he never leaves us alone. Never!

In the course of the sermon that morning, I shared some of these thoughts and experiences with the people. The sermon meant as much to me as to the hearers, and probably more. As the congregation sang the hymn of commitment, I wondered how I, newly standing in a wilderness I had never imagined, would travel the lonely path I had just mapped out for the congregation.

There was no way I could answer the question at that moment, if ever. My anger at God, so present on the trip to church, subsided as I recalled how often God had come to me in my night of nights. I knew I had not settled the issue; perhaps I never would. But it was time now to leave it on a back burner, and that's what I would do.

For now.

Chapter Eight

Although the Huntington committee missed the service, they were well represented by one committee member who was a student at a nearby seminary and had not learned of the committee's plight. Michael Queen, a young man who had been elected to the pastoral search committee and then later enrolled in Southeastern Baptist Seminary, became a committee of one and treated us to a delightful and informative lunch. I later learned he gave such a positive report to the committee's chair that the committee decided to expedite the process, eliminating their visit to North Carolina. Within days the Fifth Avenue committee had arranged for me to preach at a church some forty miles east of Huntington.

On a beautiful October morning, our family drove to Huntington, some three hundred miles north of our native state. Through beautiful mountains and softly rolling hills, we moved, as deep emotions were moving in us.

The absence of Forest was more pronounced than ever. This was our first family trip without him, and we all were crying softly. Together we wondered aloud what it would be like to live outside our home state. Family and friends would be far away.

When we met the Fifth Avenue committee, we felt an immediate connection that put to rest our concern about finding friends. Here were new friends, special people interested in us, wanting to show us their church and talk of its mission and their dreams.

I had met with many pastoral search committees over the years. Except in a few churches where pastor turnover has been too fast, there are no professional pastoral search committees. They all, thank God, are amateurs, trying their best to seek God's person for their church. The Huntington committee was exceptional in many ways. They knew what they wanted in a pastor. Our first meeting moved with dispatch as we covered the various areas of concern and responsibility on that Friday evening.

On Saturday members of the committee took us to the church, located—along with six other churches of equal size and influence—on the beautiful tree-lined street known as the "Avenue of Churches." The Baptist church, with columns like a Greek temple and reminiscent of the Parthenon, has a commanding position over the city, its front portico looking down some twenty steps onto the street.

Inside the massive edifice, the staff had gathered to meet with Faye and me. After an informative session, we were driven around the city, a beautifully planned business and residential layout initiated by Collis P. Huntington, railroad magnet and founder of the city that bears his name. That evening we had a chance to meet with the church's leadership and their spouses, the people whose talents and commitments made church happen at the corner of Fifth Avenue and Twelfth Street.

Within weeks we were back in Huntington to meet the entire congregation, or as many as would show up for what was billed as "candidating." This "trial sermon" was something of a tradition in most Baptist churches in the South. I often argued against the practice, contending that if a church hires a person on the basis of one sermon, it is naive; if it turns down a person on the basis of one sermon, it is prejudiced.

In my pastoral experience with five churches, I had preached only one such trial sermon. The other churches accepted me with sermon unheard, or as some deacon-wag once put it, "a pig in a poke pastor." In the church where I preached the trial sermon, I knew instantly when I stepped into the pulpit that this church was the place I needed to be at that time. In another church, where I didn't preach a trial sermon, I was overwhelmed when I faced the congregation on my first Sunday as pastor with the aging mass of humanity sitting before me. Had I preached a trial sermon I might have refused the church's invitation to become its pastor. But I'm glad I went there; the church blessed me and taught me as no other church could have at that point in my pilgrimage.

I, perhaps more than Fifth Avenue Church, needed the experience of candidating. I had moved rather effortlessly east and west in North Carolina, always telling God I'd go anywhere he wanted between Raleigh and Asheville. But leaving my native state? "Singing (preaching) the Lord's song in a strange land?" I didn't know. I would be moving into the American Baptist Churches, U.S.A., leaving the denomination that had spawned me and accepted my leadership locally and nationally, and going to a city described as "the most northern southern city and the most southern northern city," located where West Virginia, Ohio, and Kentucky come together on the banks of the mighty Ohio River.

As I stood in the pulpit and looked upon an expectant congregation gathered in the beautiful sanctuary, I knew immediately and without a doubt that this was my pulpit. I prayed the congregation would agree! The service was followed by an open forum, in which I answered questions put forward by the people, and then we had lunch with the committee.

During the drive home we decided that should the church call us, we would go. They did and we did.

On January 1, 1979, I told my family goodbye. We had decided Faye would remain in Hickory until we sold the house and Rachel had completed the school year. Uprooting the family in the middle of the winter was not feasible. So I headed in the car—loaded with clothes, sermon files, and books I'd need immediately—to Huntington.

Leaving my wife and daughters was the hardest thing, next to losing Forest, that I had ever experienced. We all tried to hold back the tears until we had parted. I cried so hard in the first miles on the highway I could hardly see to drive. All sorts of emotions surfaced, including mixed feelings of anger toward God over Forest's death and gratitude for the opportunity that lay before me.

As I pulled off Interstate 64 at exit 8 and made my way to the spacious house generously loaned to me by a church member wintering in Florida, a soft snow began falling. And tears came in gushes because I remembered how much Forest loved snow. When the weather forecaster predicted an overnight snow, Forest would set his clock for 4:00 A.M. so he could see the snow and get to play in it. Many times I heard him running our riding lawn mower up and down the driveway, playing in the snow. And when the predicted snow did not come, he'd wake me up and ask, "Why?"

Turning into the driveway of my "new home," I recalled that day in February, not yet a year ago, when snow had come in Hickory but soon melted.

"Dad," Forest said, as he wandered into my study. "The snow's about gone here, but they say it's really deep up at Blowing Rock. We could be there in thirty minutes. How 'bout it?"

I looked at the unwritten and overdue assignments I'd laid out for the day and then at the excitement in his eyes. "Why not?" I said, and pushed away from the loaded desk, flipped off the light, and headed toward his room. But he was already upstairs conning his mother into fixing a two-man picnic lunch.

As we drove into the mountains, the snow was getting deeper, and Forest's excitement mounted with every new inch of snow we encountered. We were both enjoying every minute. We stopped for lunch under a covered picnic table beside a half-frozen mountain stream struggling to flow, but the cold soon drove us back into the car. After driving on the most heavily snow-covered roads we could find, we headed home. Forest took a nap in the back seat as the low-lands turned snow into water.

"Dad, that was fun," he said as we unloaded our gear from car to basement. "Thanks, Dad, thanks. That was great!"

I smiled to myself through tears as snow caked on my hair while I unloaded the car. *I'm so glad I was impractical that day,* I thought, *playing in the snow rather than writing.* Being impractical at times is one of the most significant gifts parents can give children. The simple things of life, most of them costing little except time, become profound for our children.

When I asked my pastor-grandfather what he would change in his ministry if he could live it over, he said: "I'd spend more time with my children and less time with other people's." As I started to respond, he added: "Let me paraphrase a verse of Scripture: 'What will it profit you, should you become the greatest pastor in the world and be known as the world's greatest preacher, if you lose your own children?'"

Late that night I stood on the deck of my new quarters and looked over the city. I had just called my family and had completely broken down on the phone, the last thing I had wanted to do. "Why is God treating us this way?" I sobbed through the metallic lines that joined us. Once again, anger at God made its way from the back burner where I had placed it to front and center.

I'm amazed at the way hurt and anger can combine to distort reality. In my saner moments I do not believe God treats us badly. I know God wants only the best for us, even when the best is impossible for God to grant. Along with Job and his so-called comforters, we tend to believe that we did something to cause our troubles and that God's getting even with us! In such lonely hours, when the night of grief fights the morning of duty, theological perspectives from early childhood surface, and no amount of later maturing has power to hold them back. I reverted to those days of theological upbringing that instilled within me the belief, "If you do something bad, God's going to respond in like manner." In such theology, the grace of love takes a back seat to the law of retribution, a theology I had outgrown intellectually but evidently not emotionally.

In that lonely first night, I was looking back, not forward. Even when God is opening doors of new blessings, we sometimes lose the ability to take the long view. It's hard to see God's handwriting, let alone interpret what he's writing, when you're standing up to your neck in grief and anger and loneliness. In my better moments I knew that the separation from my family was only temporary, but loneliness is a tough companion, whispering all sorts of negative thoughts that can undermine faith and distort vision.

And, too, though I knew I'd make many new friends on the morrow, I was away from the support system that had nurtured me for the past four months. No one in Huntington even knew Forest. None had traveled through the wilderness with us, and I longed for fellow pilgrims who had shared the journey.

On the deck the cold air brought composure as I gazed at the lights of my new city, flickering in the falling snow. *God*, I prayed, *why have you brought me here? So far from family. So far from home. Why?* The prayer was born not out of anger or frustration but out of honest wondering. I was grateful for the opportunity offered me by the church, but I felt so small, so inadequate as I pondered what I was doing there and what God had in mind for me and the church.

No cosmic voice answered my plea, but a verse from Jeremiah surfaced: "But seek the welfare of the city where I have sent you into exile, and pray to the Lord on its behalf, for in its welfare you will find your welfare" (29:7 RSV). In all honesty, and with apologies to my Huntington friends, at that moment that's exactly what I felt had happened to me—God, as he had told his people, said also to me: "I have sent you into exile." I did feel exiled. I had lost my only son, I had left my wife and daughters three hundred miles away, and I was going from what I knew to what I knew not.

Brushing the snow from my shoulders, I entered the den, picked up the Bible, and turned to Jeremiah. I remembered something else about the prophet's twenty-ninth chapter but could not recall it completely. Then I read: "For I know the plans I have for you, says the Lord, plans for welfare and not for evil, to give you a future and a hope" (29:11 RSV).

The grandfather clock in the hall of my new residence was now striking early morning, but God's message through Jeremiah would not turn me loose. I kept reading and underlining words that now were jumping at me. I recalled the background of the passage. God's people were in exile in Babylon. Times were tough, and they were struggling with their new city. Then God gave them a blueprint for surviving and thriving in a strange and unfamiliar land: "Build houses and live in them; plant gardens and eat their produce. Take wives and have sons and daughters . . . multiply there . . . and pray to the Lord" (Jeremiah 29:5-8).

The verbs for building and maintaining community started reaching out and grabbing me: *Build, plant, produce, pray.* Home, job, family, religion—the bedrock of community. And then the promise for this preacher in a strange land: "Seek the welfare of the city . . . for in its welfare you will find your welfare."

That night the vision statement for my ministry at Fifth Avenue Baptist Church was hammered out as the city slept. On my first Sunday, five days away, I promised the people that they could expect a positive-centered pulpit, a person-centered pastorate, and principle-centered programs, all designed to "seek the welfare of the city," as God's message would be lived out within the context of the Christian faith.

With those concepts and commitments in my mind, I went to bed for the first time in Huntington as senior minister of the historic Fifth Avenue Baptist Church. The next day I would begin work as the ninth pastor in its 106 years of ministry.

But going to bed and going to sleep would not be synonymous for many months to come. That night I tried to talk with Forest. *Could he possibly be here?* I wondered. *Could he hear me?* I tried to reach over and touch him on the other side of the bed as I often did when we'd lie together on his bed and conversation and eyelids became heavy. But the space was empty.

During the early months in Huntington, living alone except for Faye's periodic visits, sometimes with the girls, I had more time than usual to think and experiment with ideas.

One of the ideas that claimed my attention, and surprised this always practical person, was dabbling in the attempt to reach departed loved ones. Such pursuits had always been off-limits to me because they were useless, in my opinion.

But I started ordering books written by people who had had out-of-body experiences, especially those authors who had experienced the "great beyond." I think I was more interested in what dying and death are like, and what heaven is like, than in trying to reach Forest. But as I reflect on those days, I believe I really felt that if I could learn from these people something about life hereafter, then somehow I might be able to contact and converse with Forest.

I dared confide in no one what I was doing. I kept the books well hidden, even from my family. This was a journey I alone would make. My mentors would stand aghast, and my peers would shake their heads, if they knew of my efforts. For many months I read book after book. But eventually I determined that I could no longer travel this road. I respected those who had had such experiences and admired their courage to share, but intellectually and theologically, I

realized, I was built differently. My experiment was over. I would
have to deal with my loss and grief in more traditional ways.

During the early days of the night of grief and the morning of
duty, which are never really separate, I learned that the mind plays
all sorts of tricks on persons struggling in grief by performing duty.
One Sunday, soon after assuming the pastorate of Fifth Avenue,
I looked high in the balcony and saw Forest! I'm glad my discovery
was during a hymn; had it been during the sermon the benediction
would have happened immediately. The young man looked exactly
like my son—same height, same build, same age. After the service
I rushed to meet him. And there stood Tim Moore, offering a
striking resemblance to Forest.

With that experience a relationship was established that continues and blesses me to this day. I did not tell Tim of the Sunday
incident until many years later. Our friendship was born of a
mistaken identity, fostered by a father missing his son and trying to
find him in some rare reincarnation. But our deepening friendship
stood on its own merit. Tim, as well as other young men the age of
Forest, became a son to me, and to Faye.

I watched Tim grow through his senior year in high school,
advised him about college opportunities, and listened carefully as
he related the growing feeling that God was calling him into the
ministry. I saw him go to seminary, helped perform his wedding
ceremony, ordained him, and celebrated with him when he became
pastor of a new church in Charlotte, N.C.

What happened in my experience with Tim verified a statement
made by Mac McGee some time after Forest's funeral. "Reinvest
your love for Forest in other people," he said. "You will find it
redemptive." I couldn't entertain such a possibility when Mac said
it, but I came to know the wisdom of his advice in the months ahead.

But just now I wanted only one thing: to talk with my son, to
hear his voice. And anger surfaced because I could not! Once again,
as I had many times during the past weeks, I asked God for Black
Chair time. My anger would subside for a spell and then surface
with intense heat. My theology told me that God knows everything,
so I assumed he knew my anger. *Why not tell him?* I reasoned.
Verbalizing my feelings, aloud and silently, became a prayer mode

that cleared the air, enabling me to function during those early months as I tried to move through the night of grief to the morning of duty. The Black Chair experience that had helped our children was now helping me.

Chapter Nine

I could sense anger growing not only in me but in Becky and Rachel, and to some degree, in Faye. But, as always, Faye was handling difficulty more effectively than the rest of the family, or so it seemed. She had had more practice.

When Faye was eight years old her father died, leaving Faye, her mother, her two brothers, six and seven, and a five-year-old sister. They were without funds. For two years Faye's mother struggled with her small brood for survival, living in an old, abandoned store on the edge of a giant tobacco farm inherited by her brother, but little real financial and family help was forthcoming.

With options to meet the daily demands of life diminishing, Faye's mother applied to the Baptist Orphanage of North Carolina. Soon all four children were housed on the beautiful campus and large farm known as Kennedy Memorial Home near Kinston, North Carolina. Faye's schoolteacher mother took a job nearby so she could be near her children.

Early in life Faye experienced the trauma of a family breaking up. Within two short years she had lost her father and her home and been separated from her mother as well as from her brothers and sister on a campus where children lived in cottages according to age and sex. Coping with such childhood challenges had equipped her to face many obstacles in life, but the loss of her son was something for which she was ill-equipped and unprepared.

In her diary, dated February 2, 1979, she confided:

It will be five months tomorrow since our son had his water skiing accident which led to his death. So much has happened; so many tears spilled.

Where are we? Where am I? I'm still searching, hurting, longing for the hurt to be just a little less. Yes, it does seem when we cry, we cry a little softer, but hurt as badly as ever. I think I've really decided I don't want that hurt to go away because when you love deeply you hurt deeply. I want only to mobilize my grief and hurt to be able to function as a healthy, well-rounded person of God, able to cope and finally reach out to other hurting people.

In her diary entry dated February 8, 1979, she wrote:

I am still at the breakfast table looking through the big picture window at one of the most scenic views in Huntington. Snow is everywhere, seven to ten inches. The bare trees hold two to three inches on their branches. The only sounds I hear are the furnace humming and the occasional chime of the hall clock.

I wake up every morning thinking about our son. Robert Forest Smith III is dead, but most of the time I say, "We LOST our son as a result of a water skiing accident." DEAD is too hard to say. I hurt deeply—all over again—every time I think of my son.

The snow seems to sadden me this morning because of the happy flashbacks of Forest in the snow with family and friends. The feeling is like a double-bladed sharp knife jabbed in the pit of my stomach. And it makes me HURT all over my body.

My son was almost too good to be true—so good, gentle, thought-ful, perceptive, unselfish, a fine Christian young man who always took time to pray and read his Bible daily. God seemed to be leading him in the area of government and his dream was to go to Washington, D.C. His memory did go to Washington to the Congressional Record in October 1978, taken there by Congressman Jim Broyhill. He read to Congress Forest's Dad's column that appeared in many newspapers, as well as Forest's essay to Wake Forest.

Faye moved more quickly into doing what Mac McGee had suggested when he reminded us to "reinvest your love for Forest." Early in her diary she wrote:

My prayer now is, "God, use me as I am to help and bless others if I am usable in accordance with your will." I've come to realize anew, she wrote, *as my husband has often said, "No experience is wasted unless we allow it to be."*

Already my life seems to be touching others I do not know, and in these long but brief months I'm beginning to put the pieces together, coming through another deep wilderness, and feel I can help people.

Faye became involved in founding the Hickory chapter of Compassionate Friends, a support group for parents who have lost children. Harriet Sarnoff Schiff addressed the group one evening, and Faye purchased her book, *The Bereaved Parent*, a volume Faye said gave her some handles for processing her grief, especially her anger. She appeared to be many miles ahead of the rest of the family, but she had become skilled in hiding hurt, something traceable perhaps to her orphanage days.

I had concern early after Forest's death about the stability of our marriage. The divorce rate of couples following the loss of a child was staggering, something like 80 to 90 percent. Few if any professional guidelines were available, or at least I was not aware of their existence. About all we knew were the statistics. They served as a warning but did little to offer guidance through the wilderness. The geographical factor in our relationship, unbeknownst to us, would have an enormous impact.

We had decided that Faye would remain with Rachel in Hickory until school was out, some six months down the road. Our plan called for Faye and Rachel to make frequent trips to Huntington, and for me to return to Hickory as often as possible. This arrangement, while difficult in many ways, proved to have a positive effect on our relationship.

Couples experiencing difficulty usually look to each other for help, at least in a healthy marriage. In our case, Faye had her support group in Hickory, and I had mine in Huntington. When we came together for a rare weekend, we came to each other in strength, not in weakness. We were not depending solely on each other for support.

In the loss of children, couples look at each other and say, though not usually verbally, "Fix it! Fix it for me. Fix me." Of course, no one person can do that for another. When the sorrow goes unfixed, the relationship suffers a blow, and after enough blows, the wounds become too severe for the relationship to endure.

I experienced this reality vividly one day when I was in bed suffering from the flu. Faye was waiting on me hand and foot, and

I was enjoying the attention and mothering even though devastated by the flu. Late one afternoon she came in, lay down on the bed, and said, "I'm afraid I'm getting your bug. I don't feel so good." Anger flashed over me. I thought but dared not speak: *What? I'm sick. This is my time to be sick, not yours. You are supposed to wait on me. You were fixing me. I can't fix you. I'm hurting too bad to fool with you. Why don't you get out of this bed and fix me?* These were honest feelings, not unlike those that couples feel toward each other when they have lost a child. The fact that Faye and I were separated but had our own support groups enabled us to avoid the pit so many couples fall into in similar situations. One of my special supporters was my in-house counselor, the Reverend Frederick O. Lewis, the young associate minister I inherited when I went to Fifth Avenue. Fred was sensitive to my loss and made himself available when he sensed I needed to talk. And that was often. Fred knew how to ask the right questions; he had a gift for creative listening and responded with precise feedback. His gentle sense of humor was a godsend for me, and he knew when to use it to lighten the load in those days of my wilderness wanderings.

But I worried about our daughters in their wildernesses. A letter from Becky soon after our first Christmas without Forest—the worst Christmas I've ever experienced—was a wake-up call that my firstborn was getting down to the nitty-gritty in her grief process. On a piece of yellow legal paper she wrote:

Dad, I can't pray. What's the use? God won't do anything anyway. He can't intervene. Verbalize our needs to psych up ourselves? Is that all it is? Where is God anyway? I don't see him acting. I see he's created our system with order and purpose and wound it up and set it loose. He won't intervene. He's made his laws and even he will not break them. Hence, we get our freedom to choose. So why pray? Why go to church except to stimulate our philosophical and moral imagination? Why should we try to live the good life when those living the bad life get the same treatment from these laws of his?

Christians are no different. In fact, I think they get screwed over more. So why believe except to assuage our consciences and curiosities about our beginnings, purpose, and end? Why not live

*in fear of nothingness after death, thus making life much more
precious? Why try to live like Christ when you know you will fail?
You can't really tell the difference between a Christian and a
non-Christian. Some of the finest people around are humanists.
Some of the most wicked and conniving I know claim Christianity.
Why even bother?*

Of course, I had heard Becky's theological complaints before.
During my student days the issues she raised had been cussed and
discussed in many a college bull session and seminary seminar. But
what my daughter wrote was not mere academic fodder for late-
night rap sessions. She was serious and her frustrations real; she
was fighting for her life and with her faith. She had lost her brother,
who was a physical and intellectual male version of her.

As I prepared a response to Becky's anger and theological
frustration, I prayed that I could give some light if not answers. I
wanted to be honest, and I didn't want to say more than I believed
or felt. I tried to convey that her questions put her in good company,
for whatever that was worth. The prophets and writers of both Old
and New Testaments had been there. And they had written honestly
about their feelings.

Jeremiah cried unto God out of his fear and pain. He almost
cursed God. Hosea was in the same boat. Job was so put out with
God that he wished he'd never been born. God's people crying over
tragedy in their personal lives and in the nation's life have left a
long trail of tears. They, too, reached the point of being unable to
pray and believe. And I've been at that crossroad many times in my
own life.

But the question comes: What is the alternative to prayer? If I do
not turn to God in my moments of defeat and tragedy, even though
I tend to blame him for my lot, to whom do I go? Where do I turn?

Becky had asked, "What's the use of praying?" Well, what's the
use of not praying? Early in my ministry I was helped greatly by
Harry Emerson Fosdick's book *The Meaning of Prayer,* in which
he deals first with the naturalness of prayer. Prayer, contends
Fosdick, is natural with us and for us. To deny this bent is to deny
the essence of our nature.

Prayer is a means of communication with our Creator, not a

magic wand to get what we want and think we need. It is a channel that deepens relationship, making us open to the inner power God can transmit to us. I think prayer also gets the molecules of our inner being pointing and moving in the same direction.

We know we use only a small percentage of our brain power and physical power. Prayer and meditation are means of opening us up toward God to such a degree that our potentials can become reality, enabling us to touch untapped resources God gave us at creation.

Prayer is a developing process through which the Creator enlivens his creation with its native and imbued powers. Becky had used the words *psych up* in her letter, and the Greek word *psyche* means "soul" or "breath." Hence, when we psych ourselves up, we are actually getting our souls in order, moving in the right direction, enabling ourselves to cope with whatever challenge confronts us.

Through prayer, the breath of God breathes into our breaths (souls) the power to cope with whatever is happening to or within us. We are spiritual persons as well as physical persons. The spirit controls the physical, and therefore prayer deals with the soul, the spirit, and provides us with a power to control the physical.

Death tears us up because we have a limited view of creation and life. God sees what we cannot see. We are limited *by* time and space *to* time and space. We don't have the framework, or points of reference, to comprehend any other life or existence beyond what we know. Our limited knowledge of God—his universe, his purpose—leaves us adrift on an uncharted sea of grief and confusion when death robs us of those we love. I doubt, however, that we could ever know enough about God to lessen the pain of losing a loved one, especially one who dies prematurely.

If we could completely understand our losses through death and tragedy, we would be God. Robert Browning is right: "Ah, but a man's reach should exceed his grasp, Or what's a heaven for?" The poet's insight gives light: If our understanding—our experience, our knowledge—were complete here and now, what need for a heaven?

Although such a theological perspective seems so much talk in times of pain, I believe we must look up from our tears as often as possible to search for scaffolding provided by those who have been through the wilderness where we now struggle. Their experiences and perspectives not only give guidance as we seek to restore life to our hurting existence but also stimulate hope, reminding us that others have made it through the maze of hurt and loss where we now find ourselves.

Admittedly, it is difficult to think such noble thoughts in the middle of the wilderness because we hurt. I encourage people to put God in his Black Chair and say, even yell, in no uncertain terms, "God, I'm hurting." Let God know it is your emptiness that cries out for fullness; it is your sorrow that begs for relief; it is your anticipated loneliness in the years ahead that weeps for your loved one to warm you with gentleness and sensitivity; it is your anger at the unfairness, injustice, and waste that causes you to shake your fist in God's face, saying that God doesn't know a thing about what he was doing with your loved one.

I did. And God took it because he knew what it was to hear his own son cry out, "My God, why have you forsaken me?" And he must have cried too.

In her letter Becky had asserted that God "can't intervene." Though I agree with her that God didn't intervene in the death of her brother, I disagree that God *could not have* intervened. God didn't intervene at the death of his son. Oh, he could have—that I believe. But he didn't. He didn't because he knew what his son would inherit, as well as what his son would give to the world. God stayed his hand because he *knew* what was in store for his son; I think he stayed his hand because he *knew* what was in store for my son.

God intervenes in history when intervention is necessary to bring about his purpose, or when a higher good for the person or humankind would be served. I must, therefore, conclude that a higher good or purpose from God's vantage point is not in the works when God does not intervene to stop the logical results of tragedies in our lives.

I guess our hang-up is at the point of seeing death as the final indignity. But God sees what we can't see; he sees death as part of the process, not an end to the process. To him it is logical; to us it is final.

Years ago I heard my pastor-grandfather tell about a man whose son had been killed. The man asked his pastor, "Where was God when my son died?" The pastor answered, "The same place he was when his son died: crying in the shadows, getting ready to receive him into his own kingdom to be with him."

That story comes back to me often. I know our loved ones have an exalted place with God, but even that faith does little to relieve suffering in the night of grief. But I must rest my case in the belief that God is love, that God loves us, that God intends only the best for us and those we love.

I'm convinced there's no way we can understand tragedy, but in the evening of death and night of grief I learned that understanding, as much as we long for it and strive for it, is not really *the* answer, maybe not even *an* answer. No amount of understanding can relieve the pain of losing a loved one, especially through a tragedy. Maybe that's the reason God does not burden us with the *why*s and *wherefore*s and *whereases*—they wouldn't help our pain anyway.

As I shared my pain and perspective with Becky, the process of dealing with my own grief was advanced a notch. I was learning that in dealing with the struggles of others, I might also find healing for myself.

Rachel's grief process took another track, just as real as Becky's but potentially more dangerous. "Dad," she said one day. "I've decided I'd like to be with Forest. I am so lonely without him."

Red flags went up all over my being. I didn't use the word *suicide*, nor did she, but we both felt the unspoken dynamic at work in her. She and Forest were born only seventeen months apart. They were close in their early days, but when Becky went off to the university they became inseparable. He was the "big brother" for her in every way. Faye and I never had to place many limits and restrictions on her—Forest was more severe in his demands of her social behavior and involvements than we were. And her respect for him, and his judgment, kept her in line most of the time. (One day she complained to me that Forest was too overbearing. "Dad," she said. "We can be at a school dance and Forest will come over and break in when I'm dancing with a boy he thinks I shouldn't be with. Will you please tell him to back off a bit?") I sensed that the loss of the security Forest had represented was frightening to her.

She was without his influence and protection. I feared what she might do in her wilderness of fresh grief.

My fear intensified when I learned she had selected for an English term paper the topic "Suicidal Tendencies in *The Bell Jar*" (a novel by Sylvia Plath). According to Rachel's outline, "certain suicidal tendencies emerge that can be identified by examining three aspects of her life: her parental associations; her internal makeup; and her external actions." In the body of her well-written paper, Rachel described a contributing factor in Plath's suicide as the death of her father. The internal factors she listed as "suicidal in general" and "mental illness," which she listed as "depression, introjection, and distorted thinking." One of the "external factors" she pinpointed was loneliness.

I read and reread Rachel's paper. The parallels were scary. Plath, whose suicidal tendencies led ultimately to suicide, wrote that following her father's death when she was eight, her childhood "sealed itself off" in something like a bell jar. Rachel's pilgrimage was too close to Sylvia Plath's for me to ignore.

Her brother, who was perhaps closer to Rachel at that time in her development as a teenager than anyone else, had died tragically, much like Plath's father (Plath believed he was the victim of murder or suicide, though in fact he had died of natural causes). But Plath's perception was reality to her. Depression was certainly a factor in Rachel's experience, as in Plath's. Lack of self-esteem, or "introjection," as Rachel labeled it, was probably operative: Rachel's self-esteem was tied in an unhealthy way to Forest, something I had been aware of for some years. And the loneliness described in *The Bell Jar* was definitely present in our youngest child's life.

Although my fears for Rachel's present and future ultimately proved groundless, I nevertheless took seriously the symptoms I perceived in her thinking at that time. In my pastoral training I was taught to recognize suicidal red flags and try to get help for people expressing suicidal sentiments. "You never smile outwardly or inwardly when a person tells you 'I want to die,'" we were cautioned. "Take all such statements as truth until proved otherwise."

I did two things: I suggested a professional counselor, to which

Rachel eagerly agreed, and I shared the several letters I had written to Forest with Rachel, as well as Becky and Faye. However, Rachel's constant contention that she'd like to be with Forest moved me to attempt a daring experiment: *to compose letters from Forest to us!* I did not take this rather extreme measure lightly. I read and reread Forest's writings and tried to get inside his style. I wrote several letters "from Forest" to the family. My main purpose was to convince our daughters, especially Rachel, that Forest was okay in his new dimension and that we should make no effort to join him prematurely.

In what some might think an off-the-wall approach, I wanted to assure Forest's sisters that what they were feeling was okay, since they could not control feelings (feelings are neither right nor wrong—they just are), and to remind them that they must control reactions to their feelings (which is something we all have responsibility for).

I wanted to share with them my belief that heaven is a life-continuing process, a time of growing toward completeness, a maturing not possible in the earthly life. But, at the same time, I wanted to emphasize that the earthly life is an important preparation for heaven's experience. The phrase from Amos 4:12, "Prepare to meet thy God," often emblazoned on concrete roadside crosses, seems better translated, "Prepare to *live* with God." Jesus often compares the kingdom of God (heaven) to a banquet to which we are invited. But we must be prepared to eat the food and participate in the conversation around the table, else we miss the joy of the feast; in short, we must prepare to *live* with God, not merely to meet God.

A friend vividly described this situation upon his return from a European trip. As a loyal member of the Rotary Club, he kept his attendance record updated by visiting Rotary clubs overseas. He related that in one club he visited, all he understood of the language was his name when they recognized him as a guest, and the food he found completely unappealing. "I was in hell," he said. "I could not understand anyone, and the food made me gag." It would be hell, I thought, to be in heaven, in the presence of God and the saints, but unable to understand the language and with no appetite for the food!

Some years ago I was in Chautauqua, New York, for a week and had the pleasure of being with the world-renowned Dr. Karl Menninger, considered the father of modern psychiatry. I had read some of Dr. Menninger's books in years past but recalled little. Had I known I would meet this fine Christian doctor, I would have brushed up on his writings so I could have conversed more intelligently with him. My experience with him was limited because my preparation for being with him was lacking. Enlarging our capacity to receive God and the things of God is a basic purpose in our earthly experience.

And I do not believe that our earthly preparation ends in heaven; rather, it increases in a more dynamic process. In the opening paragraph of one letter, Forest "wrote" that he was busier than ever as he explored heaven, which he described as "everything we ever dreamed and thought it was, and more."

My grandfather told me one day when I asked about heaven, "Son, get the greatest, most beautiful idea in your mind of what you think heaven may be like, then multiply it ten million times, and you will have only outlined a bare sketch!" I was "multiplying" my idea of heaven, hoping that somehow the process would serve to meet some of my family's questions and relieve some of their fears. As I wrote, I discovered that my own "idea" of heaven became a source of healing for me.

Over the years I've come to believe that God's plans for us are flexible. I made that belief a part of Forest's letter, shaping his letters to reinforce the idea that God did not cause the accident and to remind us that God cannot give total freedom and total security at the same time.

If God's intended plans are not possible under the circumstances, then God finds alternative plans in light of what the circumstances allow. The freedom to choose, God's gift at creation, often places us outside God's original plans for us. But God is not stymied by conditions; he reconditions his will for us in keeping with his overarching plans for us.

In the course of the letter, I felt I needed to deal with the reality of Forest's accident. He was not looking where he was going. So he recounts the accident and reckons we are angry at him for his inattention. He asks forgiveness, which everyone who loses a loved one must grant if healing is to come. Forgiveness of every person brought into the loop of blame is a step that ultimately must be taken before peace and complete healing can happen. I wanted our family to reach that level of grace. As I wrote the words, I felt such grace happening within me.

Of course, a major objective of the imaginary letter was to encourage Rachel to refocus her thinking about wanting to be with her brother. So, throughout the letter, Forest urged us not to make attempts to be with him: *Now don't get in a hurry to come here. Much as I'd like to see you, don't get in a hurry to come. God has some things yet for you four to do. I do know some of the things God has in store for you, if you will seek his will and guidance. He's not going to force them on you, but stay close to his spirit.*

People often wonder if their loved ones miss them as much as they miss their loved ones. I had Forest tell his sisters he missed them, but not in the sense they missed him. *I simply can't explain any further. You wouldn't understand, not because you are dumb, but because you don't have a point of reference to comprehend what I would say. There's nothing in all literature (including the Bible) that comes close to giving you the point of reference you'd need to understand why my missing you is different from your missing me. Just trust your big brother. Okay?*

I could say things through Forest's letters that I could not say directly to the girls. There was a mystery playing out in this process, not unlike the feeling one gets when hearing a ventriloquist communicate through the "dummy" that takes on a life of its own.

In the letters, I addressed Rachel. *I know how hard it has been for you. We were so close, especially my last three years with you. I was so proud of you—still am, talk about you here every chance I get. I know you are searching about a lot of things. Just keep on searching and looking. Things will get together for you. You've got a great head on your shoulders and feel deeply about many things. I know that. Some people do not see that in you, but it's there, and as you go through life you'll share that deep feeling with many people. And they will come to warm themselves by the fire burning in your soul.*

And to Becky, whose faith was on the verge of collapse, I could say through the letter: *I know how deeply you have searched for meaning. Your theology has been shaken, but I see you turning the corner in many ways. Doubt is okay. (God affirmed that fact to a group of us recently. He does agree with the poet that "there is more faith in honest doubt than in half the world's creeds.") But you are coming along. You will make it, and make it well. We'll have so much to talk about when that day comes for us to be rejoined. But don't get in a hurry to get here. God has some pretty exciting blasts still in store for you. Keep growing and learning. Especially about God.*

My effort to be the ventriloquist for Forest had some measure of success in our family. His "letters," read and reread, became reality for us. Later Rachel observed that they had helped redirect her desire to "be with Forest" by enabling her to move her thinking beyond the confines of her personal pain. I do not believe the letters immediately healed her. She took longer than the rest of the family in making the transition from the night of grief to the morning of duty. But reading about her brother's opinion of her backed her away from the cliff of suicide, giving her a new perspective.

I'm amazed at how God uses our clumsy efforts to help us along the road to healing. I discovered that God indeed used my writing of imaginary letters to help move us toward wholeness.

In the night of grief, the mind and soul are open to all sorts of suggestions—the good, the bad, the ugly. If we do not find ways to help people discover the good, the vacuum often is filled with the bad and the ugly. In times of grief, we will fill the void with something.

In the healing process the same procedures will not be effective for all people. Each person must row his or her own boat and become creative in finding ways to deal with the pain of loss.

Some people move to writing—prose, poetry, music. We all have gifts, and in times of weakness our strengths will often lead us to healing. Many will need support groups to ignite the spark of creativity; others will find strength and solace on a hilltop or in a meadow, maybe along a beach or perched on a high mountain. In times of crisis, Jesus alternated from seaside to mountaintop, but his purpose was the same—*to get to where God could get to him.* The old adage that "time heals all wounds" won't cut it unless we take some positive steps in the right direction. Just to sit and wait for time to heal us is fruitless. Time alone is powerless to heal. Time is opportunity; it is not answer nor solution.

Nothing "just happens." We must make things happen, especially in the first year following loss. We must set in motion positive pursuits; get into a position and condition for the Holy Spirit to aid in the mobilizing process of grief; make ourselves available to the prevailing winds of God's Spirit. "They serve, too, who sit and wait" is not an apt description of positive motion in the grieving process. Time is but God's gift that must be opened so proper resources can be permitted access into our lives.

Though I encourage persons not to make major decisions during the first year following loss, I do encourage them to mobilize in ways that are possible in the face of their grief and pain.

To people facing personal or business crises, and especially the trauma of loss, I have suggested what I call the Four-D Process.

First: *Define the issue.*

Sometimes the "D" may spell discovery; that is, you must discover the real issue facing you before you can define it. In the loss of a mate, the issue may well be financial fear. "How will I survive?" "How will I put bread on the table and keep the house?" Many times the issue needs to be admitted, not discovered.

A friend became extremely depressed immediately following the funeral service of her husband. A few days later she admitted to me, rather timidly and with mixed feelings, that she worried about not having enough financial resources to sustain her. "I know this is unchristian to worry about such things so soon after my husband's death," she said. "But I don't know what I will do." I assured her that fear for her financial future was logical, given the circumstances, and had nothing to do with being Christian or unchristian.

A few days later she brought to my office an overstuffed folder of papers. "We don't have much in the bank, but my husband used to tell me that this folder would be all I'd ever need. I don't know what he meant." The file was filled with stock certificates! I referred her to a stockbroker who established that she could live far beyond her life expectancy and never exhaust her resources.

Discovering and defining the issue often is half the solution.

Second: *Develop a philosophy or theology of the issue.*

For instance, early in my ministry I recognized that I could never take a vacation and stay home. When I was in the community, I was available, regardless of my intention to relax and do nothing. When a crisis arose, I was called and I responded, vacation or no vacation. I knew the only way to be truly on vacation was to get out of town. Once I developed that component in my theology of ministry, I could make the necessary accommodations to implement it.

When we lose a loved one, we know that life can never be the same. To pretend otherwise is to "whistle in the dark." Business as usual is not a healthy option. To tell ourselves that "time will heal me" or "he's not really gone" is an exercise in futility, and we might as well, in the words of my grandmother, "save your breath to blow and cool your coffee."

The philosophy must deal with what is normal in a given situation, what is abnormal, what is negotiable, what is nonnegotiable, what are my short-term goals, what are my long-term goals, what sacrifices will I make, and what sacrifices will I refuse to make.

Third: *Design a structure to express and carry out the philosophy.*

This process involves identifying one's native talents in light of the philosophy, and the time and energy available. People have different thresholds of physical pain. And this is also true with emotional pain. Some people can endure extreme pain, especially the pain of loss. They have a talent, it seems, to work quickly and effectively with the loss of a loved one. But each person must work with the talent of coping that he or she possesses.

Fourth: *Dedicate oneself to the structure.*

The saying "Plan your work and work your plan" has merit. In the course of dealing with loss, a person must have a plan that will enable progress to happen. I believe that what is planned is possible.

Actually, the person who has no plan has a plan, and it is a plan that promises disaster. Nature indeed abhors a vacuum. All sorts of unwanted demons fill the void that comes from a no-plan posture. My father was eighty-one years old when my mother died. Dad lived alone in the family country home. Living over three hundred miles from him, I was concerned about his welfare. But he was coping beautifully. One day I asked how he managed to deal with the vacancy Mom's death had created for him. "Structure, Son, structure," he said. "I structure my days. I make plans, and I make my plans work for me. I get up at a certain time and make my breakfast (two fried eggs, three pieces of bacon, two pieces of toast and jelly, plus coffee). Then I go to my workshop and work on whatever project I've got going. I mow grass, rake leaves, trim hedges, or do whatever else needs doing around the grounds. In the afternoons I run errands."

As I pondered Dad's life after his loss, the formula for surviving (and thriving) came into focus: *Structure gives stability, and stability gives security.* Security is the result of good planning and appropriate implementation of the plan. And security expands horizons, opens new doors, and gives birth to a spirit of adventure as one moves to the morning of duty.

Part 3

The Morning of Duty

"And on the next morning I did
as I was commanded." (Ezekiel 24:18b)

Chapter Ten

Making the morning of duty a reality was more difficult than I had imagined. The evening of death could be identified fairly clearly. It began when we knew Forest could not survive the accident, intensified at 1:05 A.M., Tuesday, September 12, the moment he died, and ended sometime after the funeral, perhaps the next day when the crowd had scattered and we were alone.

Then the night of grief was in complete control. Even in the evening of death, we sensed that night was coming. For days before Forest died we could feel grief struggling for birth in the womb of our souls. The evening of death had a certain closure, although the line of demarcation was somewhat jagged, zigzagging in and out.

But no such line marked the end of night's grief and the dawn of morning's duty. Grief and duty joined hands, coloring each other's moments, yet supporting each other as life moved on but with a different emphasis on every moment and decision.

Ezekiel's literary leap from evening to morning, skipping the night, was making sense. The night and morning, I was learning, were so intermingled that no separation of the two was possible. I became convinced that Ezekiel's morning of duty and the night of grief he never talked about were really one and the same. After all, evening covers from about sundown to somewhere around midnight. And midnight ushers in the morning.

As I tried to analyze the evening, the night, and the morning with the tool of chronos, I realized that the only way I could deal with the dilemma was to accept kairos. While night and morning are marked by chronos (time to get up, shower, shave, dress, go to work, all measured by clock time), the whole experience of dealing with grief was a kairos experience. I could not clock my crying times or my hurting times or my times of thinking about Forest. They invaded every waking moment, unsolicited, uninvited, and often unwelcome.

Early one morning I was driving to the office and heard myself say aloud, "Six months today." Then I muttered, "Seems like six hours." But another part of me argued, "No. More like six years!" According to my chronos calendar, Forest had died six months ago that day. But according to my feelings (my kairos), the time elapsed seemed somewhere between hours and years.

Why does grief produce such a confusion of time? I wondered. As I drove along with morning mists slowly soaking into the sun's sponge, I reasoned that time seems short or long because we actually live three days for every one day when in deep grief.

We live each day *the way things were.* We recall how life used to be: the tender moments, the joys, the whole mix of experiences telescoped into each day. Memories, as warm and tender as they are, nevertheless produce pain, a longing for what once was but never can be again. That hurts and generates a vividness that prolongs the past, making it almost present.

And we live each day *the way things are.* Reality must become real—jobs to go to, other lives to touch, meals to cook, houses to clean, oil to change in the car, and dozens of other real things to do. Yet doing these reality things jars memory of things past and kicks up feelings that lengthen hours into days of suffering, confusing the passage of time until one wonders what is reality and what is not.

Then we live each day *the way things could have been.* This is the hardest, most difficult day of all, a day confused by dreams: "We could have done this together." "He would have liked this." "We could have gone to that play." "We could have done this . . . and . . . this . . . and that . . . *if, what if, if only.*"

The days are sometimes like hours, sometimes like years, and sometimes not like anything because grief makes reality hard to grasp, makes it so . . . unreal.

I had reached my chronos destination. I parked but sat for a long time in the car because my kairos would not turn loose. I prayed that the Great Physician would somehow anoint me with a healing salve. I prayed silently, *O Lord, when will the three days become one? When will the past and future not burden my present? When will they become what they really are—past and future?* As I finally turned off the car's engine I came to a conclusion: *I have buried my son's future. I will not bury his past.*

That commitment became one of the most strategic tools I had for moving more fully into my morning of duty. I reasoned that I would not bury our daughters' pasts even though their babyhoods and childhoods were dead. Forest, too, had a past. I resolved that I would talk about all three, recall their days of yesteryear, and frolic in the good times we had had during those years. *Forest's past is as alive as theirs,* I decided silently.

One of the mistakes families often make is refusing "to speak of the dead." But they overlook a vital tool available to those who are going through the night of grief.

I accidentally stumbled upon a pastoral tool when I first went to Fifth Avenue. A large percentage of the congregation at that time was elderly. I conducted the funerals of many people I did not know; most of them I had never seen. In an effort to make the memorial service personal, I would ask the family to assemble at a given time so I could talk with them. But I really wanted them to talk to me. I would say, "I'd like for each of you to give me five words that come to mind when you think of _____" (citing whatever name or relationship described the deceased person).

This conversation helped me a great deal in preparing the service, but I soon discovered that such sessions had tremendous therapeutic value for the family. They would begin with words at first. Then they'd move to sentences and paragraphs and ultimately entire scenes. They'd tell humorous incidents that caused the gathering to burst into laughter. Then would come some tender and sad story that moved them back to tears. In some situations family members were not speaking to each other, and hadn't for years. But as the family shared together—the good, the bad, the in-between times—walls of separation were penetrated, and in some cases completely torn down.

I recall one situation in which two brothers had not spoken to each other in years. After an hour of sharing, I saw the older brother rise from his seat, go over to his younger brother, and embrace him as their tears intermingled. The whole family almost shouted at the moment of reconciliation. One of the brothers told me recently that when they shared the past he and his brother had had together, he could not bear to live the present or face the future without his brother. Although we cannot live again in the past, the past can live again in our present.

Today—the present—offers two opportunities: First, we can turn loose of yesterday's negatives, once we learn from them. And second, we can relive in memory incidents of the past that continue to enrich our lives.

I learned about reliving happy experiences during my first pastorate after seminary. One afternoon I dropped by to visit Miss Flossie, as the little town affectionately called her, a retired schoolteacher who had lived into her nineties, a fact no one dared mention to her. She was sitting alone in her den with albums of photographs spread before her and all over the place.

"What are you doing?" I asked.

"I'm just sitting here thrilling," she said, lifting her head and looking up over her reading glasses.

"Doing what?" I asked again, not certain I had heard her correctly.

"*Thrilling*," she emphasized. "Just thrilling over my memories," she said. And she waved her hand over the hundreds of photos scattered around the room.

Then she explained to her young pastor that she and her late husband had taken a world cruise upon retirement. Her eyes cleared and her face became a smile as she recalled those days of the past that had come momentarily to live in her present. Holding up a large picture of the cruise ship they had enjoyed so much, she said, "The most wonderful thing about memories is that you can live them again and again and again." After a brief visit, I left Miss Flossie thrilling over her memories. In the years ahead I came to know the truth of her perspective.

Memories with Forest surfaced in detail as I recalled experiences that both hurt and healed at the same time. I could not yet thrill, as did Miss Flossie, over the memories I was reliving. The warm memories generated hot tears in those early days. Months of healing were required before perspective would allow the thrill to thrill. At that time I had no way of knowing when the night of grief would give way to a definite morning of duty.

Again and again I almost yelled at God in some of our Black Chair sessions, "How long is this terrible night of grief? When will it be over? When will I quit hurting?" Hundreds of people have aimed that question at me over the years. And I've never found a satisfactory answer. Perhaps the only real answer is a question given me by a man laying carpet in our living room shortly after we moved to Huntington. As I watched him expertly stretching and fastening the carpet to the floor, I ventured a question, more to make conversation than to gain information. "How long will the carpet last?" I asked.

He paused, rose up on his knees, and said, "Well, I don't want to sound smart-alecky, but let me ask you a question. How many bites in a sandwich?"

I smiled and nodded my head as we both stared at each other. "Gotcha," I finally said, and he smiled the smile of a good teacher, hit his flat carpet tool on his blue-jeaned thigh, making a slapping sound like a period placed after a sentence of absolute reality, then turned again to his carpet job.

And I turned my thoughts to the wisdom of a carpet layer who had laid on me a truth I would need to work through. I knew that I alone could decide how many bites in my sandwich. And I was beginning to realize that I alone would decide how long would be my night of grief. As I wandered back to my study, I knew that coping with the morning of duty would ultimately push back the night of grief. And I had to get on with it.

My morning of duty was getting under way as I took up the mantle of pastoral leadership at Fifth Avenue Baptist. I determined that during my first year I would concentrate on three projects: preaching, teaching, and getting to know the people. The last would be my biggest and most important challenge. I had a barrel of sermons and files of lecture notes to draw from, but trying to meet and get to know seven hundred families would demand tremendous energy. But it was precisely while using enormous amounts of energy in getting to know my people that healing gained a solid foundation so I could begin to turn loose my hold on the night. Turning loose of the night was not as easy as it sounds, however. There was a sense of guilt when I started feeling better after the loss of Forest. When humor played around in my mind, occasionally slipping out spontaneously, I would remember my dead son and feel bad that I felt good. The longer I could hold onto Forest, the more real was my love, or so I felt. And any statement, however veiled or positioned, suggesting that I needed to turn loose and get on with life, met with hostile resistance.

One day during my early weeks at Fifth Avenue, Leland Bunch, a faithful member who had a deep sense of responsibility for the elderly in the church, asked that I accompany him to visit one of our oldest members. Miss Lois, as the younger generations called her, pulled no punches, regardless of the issue up for discussion. We soon got by the usual platitudes of first meetings and moved on to heavier stuff. "Tell me about your family," she said, delivering more an order than a request. She was genuinely interested in her new pastor's family and soon adopted us as her family, teasing my wife by claiming to be "his new girlfriend."

But she almost missed being any kind of friend for me. While telling her about my family, I evidently talked too long about Forest to suit her. "Listen, young man," she said, and her eyes were spitting fire. "Turn that boy loose! You can't hang onto him forever. He's dead and he's gone, and all your talking and crying will not bring him back. It will just make you worse. You've got two daughters who need you. They need your best. Turn Forest loose; let him go. Give your time to your family and to this church that needs you more than you realize. You've got to turn that boy loose."

I don't remember what I said in response to her lecture. But I wanted to punch the old gal in the nose. I was never so angry at a person in all my life. As Leland and I drove back to my office, I remember mumbling that she didn't have a right to say what she had said. As I dashed into my office, I waved at my associate, motioning for him to come in and close the door.

For the next thirty minutes I ventilated my anger before Fred Lewis, whose facial expressions and silence were just what I needed to help me deal with a truth that had been thrown upon me in no uncertain words. When Fred left, I wheeled my chair toward the window as traffic whizzed by on busy Fifth Avenue, and with some degree of composure I recalled that Jesus said, "You shall know the truth and the truth shall make you free." Expanding his statement to include "truth in general," I could well add: "and the truth shall make you angry at times!"

Did it ever! Of course, what Miss Lois said was true. Should she have said it? Maybe. Maybe not. At the time, I felt she was off base, out of line, and sticking her nose where she had no business. But looking back, I realize I needed to hear what she said. After all, I was several months into the night of grief. In my saner, more honest moments, I knew she was right. Her statement and the carpet man's "How many bites in a sandwich?" were challenging me, maybe beginning to move me.

Only weeks later did I learn Miss Lois had lost a son. So long ago not many people remembered. Maybe she did have the right to say what she said. At least, she had the experience. She had confronted me, rather harshly, I felt. As I licked my wounds during the next few days, I remembered that in my theology of church I had contended the church has four tasks in ministry with people: oftentimes to *confront*, sometimes to *correct*, at all times to *comfort*, but never at any time to *coerce*. Miss Lois had implemented two of the church's tasks—she had confronted and corrected, or at least set the stage for a course correction. She had almost coerced, but not quite.

In the night of grief most of us know how to comfort, but most of us are not comfortable doing what Miss Lois did. In fact, knowing how to confront, in the hope of correcting, is a skill more innate than we admit, and most of us can do it well. But the *how* is not so important as the *when*. If we confront too early, the person is devastated, and correction is impossible.

Some time ago a couple who had lost their teenage son were referred to me by their physician. They were only four weeks into their night of grief as they sat in my office hurting. I listened and asked a few leading questions that enabled them to dump everything out on the table. Devoted members of their church in a neighboring city, they told me that two weeks after their son's funeral, their pastor told the mother on her way out of church, as she wiped her tears, "You have got to get beyond this. This is no way for a Christian to act. Turn him loose. He's better off where he is than we are. Get beyond it." That was their last trip to church. And I understand why. Confronting a grieving person too early is as cruel as it is counterproductive. Knowing when to say the right words that will move to positive action takes the skill of an artist and the insight of a prophet.

But there are some guideposts along the way. I'm often asked, "How long will the fresh grief last?" I could answer, "How many bites in a sandwich?" But that would be too cruel, at least in the valley of fresh grief. In my experience, sensitive grief begins to lessen in about six to twelve months. If at the end of a year the person is grieving in the same way as in the week of death, professional counseling is indicated. Delayed grief, that is, delayed processing of grief, can have serious consequences. The night of grief is not something we can take lightly. Many times people cannot get through the night on their own. Expert counselors are often needed.

"Getting over" the death of a loved one and "going through" the experience of losing a loved one are not the same. I doubt we ever "get over" a loss. But we can "go through" it.

I often compare the loss of a loved one to the experience of abdominal surgery. When I was in my late twenties, I had major surgery. For the first few days and weeks after the surgery I guarded the long scar on my stomach while taking a shower with the intensity of a SWAT team on alert. I dared not let the water hit the scar. As weeks turned to months, I guarded the scar with less intention. About a year following the operation, I no longer protected the wound. The scar tissue was firm, insulating sensitivity, making showers normal. I haven't forgotten, however, that one day I was cut open, that for weeks the incision hurt and needed protection. The scar is still there. I saw it this morning as I showered. I will never *get over* the surgery. The scar won't let me forget. But I did get beyond it.

The emotional experience of losing a loved one is not too

different from having a physical operation. Both are surgery. They take from us something that was real and important. And the *taking* hurts. The recovery is terrible. In the course of a year the formation of scar tissue should enable us to function again. But the scar constantly reminds us of that day when we lost someone who was more precious than life itself. We will never get over loss, but we will get on the other side of it.

Getting *over* the death of a loved one is not the issue; getting *through* it is the only thing that counts. My grandfather, the Reverend H. S. Benfield, set this thought in my mind when I was a little boy. Papa, as his nine children and all the family called him, was a best friend to me as well as my pastor. Often I would accompany him on pastoral visits.

One day we called on a family who had lost a loved one. Papa talked and listened to them for a while, then opened the family Bible. He chose Psalm 23. He read the great old psalm with deep feeling, bringing comfort along with tears. When he had finished reading, he looked at the grieving family and said, "The most important word in this psalm for you just now is the little preposition *through*. The psalmist reminds us that we shall not remain forever in this valley of the shadow of death. We will go through it. In time. Not now, but one day, someday in the future you will go through it. And you're not alone. The Good Shepherd of the sheep is with you. He will never leave you alone." Later, in my own study of Psalm 23, I underlined that preposition *through* in all my Bibles.

Papa's theology and interpretation of Psalm 23 haunted me at times. But eventually I came to know the reality of the old pastor's wisdom.

I knew the past could not heal until it passed, because the past is not past until it has passed. And, God knows, I was working at it, sometimes moving forward three steps, then sliding back two. But that was progress.

Chapter Eleven

The length of grief's night, and our progress in going through it, may well be determined by how effectively we resolve anger over the death of the loved one. Three facts about anger demand serious attention: First, loss produces anger; second, anger must be admitted; third, anger must be expressed if it is ultimately to be resolved.

In my four-plus decades as a pastor working with grieving persons, I have observed that anger is so off-limits in matters of faith that people delay healing by refusing to admit it. In the eighteen years since Forest's death, dozens of parents in similar circumstances have found their way to my office. Some were members of my church, but most were from other churches and religious traditions, referred by physicians, counselors, and clergy. In almost every case their anger was denied. "Getting mad at God" was, in their theology, taboo—a denial of faith, something they dared not admit. One of the main goals in our sessions was to uncover the anger, bring it to the surface, lay it on the table, and let them learn that anger at God is okay.

Some years ago a prominent minister and his wife, both good friends of ours, were visiting with us over the weekend. They had lost a son many years ago in a tragic accident. We were talking about our sons and our losses. I told them about my anger at God the night our son died. Then I ventured a question: "How did you deal with your anger toward God?" The wife flew into a rage. "What do you mean?" she fairly shouted. "Never! I have *never* been mad at God because our son died," and her eyes flashed darts as her body trembled with emotion.

I did not challenge her. She had lived with that anger for years; I would not disturb her defense mechanism. Had I been counseling with her, my response would have been different. After they left, my wife said, "You really stirred up a hornets' nest with her. She's still mad at God."

Unadmitted anger stays around a long time and infects life, often destroying many good things that could bless and enrich life. Anger is an emotion, a feeling. And we cannot help our feelings. When someone hits you, you feel pain. Any philosophy, theology, and theory you can muster will not keep you from feeling the pain. You cannot help *feeling the feeling*. Feeling is neither right nor wrong; it just is.

What you *do* about the feeling is a matter of choice—appropriate or inappropriate responses, positive or negative reactions. We are not responsible for our feelings, but we are accountable for our actions. Emotions are neither moral nor immoral, but how we deal with them is a matter of moral responsibility.

When death strikes your loved one, you feel the pain of loss. A real and natural part of that loss is the feeling of anger. Anger is reaction to pain and becomes pain, taking on a life of its own. Often, even when the wound of fresh grief is protected by a scar, anger remains beneath the surface, irritating and preventing total healing. Some people's anger continues for years, preventing them from completely reentering life.

Some people cannot return to their relationship with God, and they never darken the doors of their community of faith again. But the unresolved anger toward God still haunts them and hinders their complete recovery. Unless anger is monitored and properly processed, it becomes more deadly than the loss that caused it. Admitting anger, especially at God, is not heresy. It is a healing step; it is trust in action, the belief that God not only understands but cares.

I daresay Mary and Martha were angry at Jesus when their brother Lazarus died. They had sent for Jesus to come when they discovered Lazarus was sick. But Jesus did not come immediately. When he did come, both Mary and Martha leveled their frustration at him—tinged perhaps with anger: "Lord, if you had been here, my brother would not have died" (John 11:21, 32 RSV).

I turned Mary and Martha's frustrated declaration into an angry question and leveled it at God in our Black Chair confrontation.

"Where were you, God? Had you been here tending to business my son would not have died." Though my Black Chair session that first night diffused my immediate anger at God, I was not entirely out of the wilderness of anger.

Several weeks later while studying the Gospel of John, I came to chapter 11 and the incident about Lazarus. As Jesus approached Lazarus's tomb, some of the friends asked: "Could not he who opened the eyes of the blind man have kept this man from dying?" (John 11:37 RSV). I underlined that question. Through tear-blurred eyes I wrote in the margin of my Bible, "How about Forest, also?" For weeks I could not get beyond that verse of Scripture; that pricking, prodding question that caused my insides to roll—not in faith—but in anger.

The question "Why do bad things happen?" fades into the philosophical background when you raise the theological question: "Could not God have kept this bad thing from happening?" Your faith makes you answer, "Yes, Jesus could have kept him from dying." Then you expand that answer—if you believe in the all-powerfulness of God—to say, "And he could have kept *my loved one* from dying!" That makes all the questions harder. And that question, "Why didn't God prevent it?" kept me grazing and gazing in a back pasture much longer than I wanted. I couldn't get away from it. I could not move on.

Such questions scream at us from delivery rooms when little babies come into the world minus normal limbs and organ systems; when we stand on military battlefields, complete with monuments marking bravery, and crosses and stars marking graves of the country's finest; when the ravages of age cripple bodies beyond recognition; when hunger and disease and hatred and pestilence and earthquakes and tornados and plane crashes and ships sinking and terrorists' bombs combine to bring pain and loneliness and devastation, we cry, "My God, why?" And, "My God, why not stop it?"

With Lazarus's mourners, we ask, "Could not he have kept this man from dying? Could not he have kept these tragic things from happening?" We answer yes. Then we ask, "Why didn't he?" We can give some answers. Maybe.

God cannot violate his own principles, we can say, not even to keep our loved ones safe. Perhaps granting recovery does not serve God's purpose for our loved ones, we pontificate. We can safely say God sees what we can't see and knows what we can never know this side of heaven. Maybe then we shall know; perhaps then we shall understand. But all this really doesn't help much, does it? It's too logical, too theological, too thin to cover our wounds, and too mild to effect much healing.

These questions and feelings produce anger, mostly because we cannot answer or explain the unexplainable and the unanswerable. Dr. Bill Sheils Sr., our family's physician, told me that a traveling family stopped at the hospital where he was on emergency room duty one night to get help for their mother, who was gravely ill. The medical staff did what they could, but she died in spite of their efforts.

The task of telling the large family the sad news fell to Dr. Sheils. As sensitively as possible, he told them their mother had passed away. There was stunned silence. Then one of the sons, the size of a professional football interior lineman, got up and took a swing at the doctor, who fortunately ducked the punch as the man's fist went through a door.

Anger is real when we lose loved ones. And we look around for someone or something to hit. Sometimes it's the medical staff. Or the hospital (most of which have faced lawsuits testifying to anger). Or the system of government that doesn't keep highways safe or do enough to prevent crime. Often we simply get mad at the universe that permits accidents.

After losing Forest, I experienced an anger I'd never had before. One day I was driving home and saw a young man, about Forest's age, thumbing a ride on the outskirts of the city. He was a bum by every standard applied. I became angry at him. *Why is he wasting his life? Why is he living and my son's not? Forest had a brilliant present and a wonderful future. This guy is a loser.* It was Black Chair time again. "Tell me," I was saying aloud. "Just tell me what justice you see in all of this. This guy lives and breathes and walks around doing nothing. Forest was on target. He had his head on straight. Why let a bum like that live and let Forest die? Why? Tell me that!"

I wondered if other people experienced similar feelings, so in counseling sessions I carefully crafted questions to determine if perhaps others felt resentment when they saw a person wasting life while their loved one's life had been cut short. Almost to a person, each had had such feelings and secretly asked the same angry questions. I discovered the importance of stimulating each person to admit such anger, as well as to ventilate it. One father, who had lost a little daughter, confided that he became angry at fathers who were spending little or no time with their children. "I want to grab them, shake them, and tell them what they ought to be doing," he said as tears filled his eyes.

Many times the earliest anger is at self. "What did I do to cause this?" Or, "How could I have kept this from happening?"

For months I beat myself over the head because I did not tell Forest to come home. He and I had planned to hit a few golf balls late in the evening before barbecuing dinner. He had asked permission to stay a little longer skiing on the lake. I could have prevented the accident, I told myself over and over, by speaking three words: "No, come home." Forest would have obeyed. But I didn't speak those words. Now I could never have him home again. Never. And I was angry at myself.

But the hardest anger to admit, maybe even more difficult than admitting anger at God, is confessing anger at the lost loved one.

Becky's turning point in healing came when she ventilated her anger at her brother, fairly shouting, "Why in the devil didn't Forest look where he was going? If he had been paying attention to what he was doing, we would not be in this hell that's killing us!" Saying aloud her deep feelings of resentment was difficult. But her feelings were real, justified or not. Getting the feelings on the table where she and the family could acknowledge them was therapeutic.

Such honesty is hard to express, but it is a vital step in resolving anger and effecting healing. Blaming the dead loved one, even when the cause of death is definitely of their making, is difficult because we've been taught never to speak ill of the deceased. But the anger is there, admitted or not. And healing often begins when anger at the deceased is finally brought out of the closet and openly expressed.

"He brought this on himself," said a young daughter as we stood over the casket of her father who had died all too early. "His smoking," she said. "He knew the dangers. We talked about it often. Our family did everything possible to encourage him to stop smoking. But he used to laugh and say, 'I won't die until my time comes,' and that ended all discussion." I watched as she beat the back of a chair in anger at her father's unwillingness to take life seriously.

"He drank himself to death, you know," grieving wives have told me over the bodies of their husbands. Others have accused dead loved ones of overwork, driving while too tired, poor diets, not taking medicine, and a multitude of negative lifestyles that brought on too-early deaths. Admitting anger at loved ones who contributed to their early deaths is therapeutic. Such anger must be resolved before healing can take place.

Even when the loved one's death was of natural causes, and they were in their autumn years, some survivors experience a feeling of abandonment. They become angry because "he left me all alone." "What will I do without her?" generates all sorts of angry and negative feelings toward the deceased loved one.

When I admitted and expressed my anger at God, I discovered that admitting my anger toward persons and circumstances became easier. Private admission and expression of anger is important, and a first step. But expressing the anger in the presence of another person is most therapeutic. Of course, care in selecting the person to whom one admits and expresses anger is crucial. Flinging angry feelings on whoever is available is too often counterproductive because not all people can handle another's anger, especially toward God. I suggest seeing a professional counselor or a pastor who has had counseling training.

Although anger at God is hard to admit, let alone express, confessing our feelings to God becomes a worship experience and the ultimate exercise in prayer. After all, real prayer is being honest with God and before God. As a friend once observed, "Prayer is loading all your feelings, fears, frustrations, hopes, and desires into a large dump trunk and dumping them before the throne of God, and letting God sort out and deal with them as he sees fit." Maybe that's what "asking in his name" means. That could be the essence of "not my will but thy will be done."

If we believe God knows everything, then God knows our anger. So why not admit it? Why not express it? Frankly, I believe we don't express anger toward God and other people effectively because we've been told not to all our lives. Parents constantly program children: "Don't get mad. Nice girls and boys don't get angry. Now be a good boy; be a good girl." With this approach parents are teaching the art of denying basic emotions. When we tell our sons that "big boys don't cry," we are misleading them and setting in motion certain patterns that are likely to render them incapable of expressing all emotions, including love. Our parental task is to teach children how to handle emotions, not deny them. Especially anger. We need to guide them in what to do with anger and how to mobilize the emotion creatively.

And any anger toward God is definitely off-base, we've been told. As one parent said, "If you get mad at God, for goodness sake don't let him know it."

But unresolved anger is dangerous. It locks up good emotions and too often releases bad ones. People become bitter and pessimistic when anger is not properly resolved. In fact, most of the bitterness we experience with people is nothing more or less than unresolved anger.

Just before retreating to complete the last chapters of this book, I was contacted by a person deeply concerned about two of her relatives, a mother and father who had lost a son. For two years since their loss they had progressively retreated into themselves. They refused to interact with people and had grown increasingly bitter at the world. When I suggested a capable counselor, the relative told me they refused to talk with anyone about their situation. "They have cut everyone out of their lives," she said. Such a situation often develops when anger is unresolved. People become hermits, nurturing their anger until it effectively imprisons them.

The other day I inquired of the whereabouts of a certain child. The mother said, "He's hiding behind his anger." Perhaps we adults do the same. Anger is an excellent means for isolating ourselves from God, people, and reality. While I was intensely angry with my

Creator, I came to realize that God was trying to get through to me, but my anger had become a fortress. My anger began subsiding, even finding resolution, when I started dealing with the haunting question: "Where is God in all of this?" I would not find many answers; I cannot to this day make sense of it. But there came a time when I had to back off and take a long look at God and try to formulate some workable ideas that would enable me to live without answers to some of life's hardest questions.

Did God cause the accident that took Forest's life? Was his death God's will? No mortal being can give definitive answers to such ancient questions. But I do have some beliefs and concepts that nurtured me as I coped with his death.

First, God did not cause the tragedy. We are free human beings, and we choose what we want to do. And we live in a world where accidents are possible, even probable. Put freedom of choice and an accident-prone world together, and you have potential tragedy.

Forest had an accident while doing something he loved. Water skiing is dangerous, yes. But so is almost everything we do. The only way to avoid such accidents is to take no risks in life. And this would produce prisons where we would die of physical, mental, emotional, and spiritual malnutrition.

I believe that God, who loves our son and each of us, did not *will*, did not desire, that his life be cut short after only seventeen years. Yet being free to live in a world where accidents can produce death, our son met such an accident. God did not cause it; God did not will it. It happened, accidentally.

God, however, in love and wisdom, did not allow this tragedy to be wasted. God stepped into the middle of this tragedy and brought good out of it. I have seen good things coming from the accident for nearly two decades. God has a way of taking shattered dreams and making something new, something real, from the brokenness.

Second, nothing in God's world is broken beyond any hope of repair. Although God does not repair the brokenness of our loved one's tragedy, he does repair our lives so we can live again, laugh again, and love again. I believe, as a fellow minister wrote in a letter shortly after Forest's death, that "God's participation at the point of cause may not be a good question for you and me to ask, but God's participation at the place of resolution—healing, strengthening—is a good question and we can find God."

His concluding sentence is most powerful: "We find God not at the cause but at the cure."

Chapter Twelve

My pilgrimage now moved from discovering God at the point of cause to finding God at the point of cure. The demands of a new pastorate were enabling me to write new chapters in my life. Yet something was missing. Mac McGee had stressed over and over the need "to reinvest your love." I was trying. Meeting a new church family, getting to know them, feeling loved by them as I came to love them, was meeting more needs than I had dared imagine.

But there was a part of me not being reinvested.

One afternoon I was driving by Marshall University, only four blocks from the church, with Jim Cox. Jim had served as vice chair of the pastoral search committee and had become my tour guide and meal companion in the early months in Huntington. We saw the football team practicing, getting ready for their fall encounters.

"Jim," I said. "Right there's something I'd like to do," and pointed to the football players.

"What? Play football?" he teased.

"No. I'd just like to be around those boys. They are about the same age as Forest. I don't know what I could do, but I would like to hang out with them some."

I made that statement on Wednesday. The following Sunday during coffee time in the old fellowship hall of Fifth Avenue, Dave Pancake, who later became a friend and our family's attorney, pulled me aside.

"Sonny Randall, the new football coach at Marshall, wanted me to ask if you'd consider becoming chaplain of the football team." I was speechless, a matter Dave interpreted as resistance to the idea. "You don't have to answer now. Just think about it," he encouraged.

"No, Dave, you don't understand." Then I told him of the

conversation with Jim Cox only three days ago. "I can't believe this," I said.

Coach Randall had evidently visited the community churches looking for a pastor to become his team's chaplain. "You're the pastor he wants if you'll agree," Dave was relating, as I tried to compute the speed of what was happening.

"Tell the coach to call me and we'll discuss it over lunch," I said.

The next day Coach Randall called. Over lunch we started getting to know each other. I knew Sonny Randall by reputation. He had played for the University of Virginia before going to the National Football League. There he had played for eleven seasons, mainly with the St. Louis Cardinals. While there he was designated "All Pro" four times. After his pro career he had coached at East Carolina University, and then at the University of Virginia, his alma mater.

Marshall University had invited him to come and rebuild its football program, which had been devastated in 1970 when a chartered airplane crashed on landing at the Huntington airport on a foggy, rainy night. All seventy-five people aboard were killed: thirty-seven football players, eight coaches and staff members, the plane crew, and a number of community leaders. The university, as well as the city, had struggled for nine years to rise from the ashes of this tragedy.

"I'm going to need some strong help if I do what they've hired me to do," Sonny said, and his eyes were intense and serious.

"What do you want a chaplain to do?" I asked.

"I want him to be a part of the team, help the team become a family, and become totally involved in the lives of the players and coaches."

I told Sonny I would refuse to be simply window dressing for the team. If he would give me total access to the team and coaches, allowing me input into developing relationships, calling things as I saw them, I'd be honored to be a part of his team.

"You will have a green light into all phases of our program," he promised. "No door will be closed to you." Sonny Randall kept his promise, even during some difficult days when the local and national press gave him and the team a hard time. Sonny had his critics, but to me he became a brother, a relationship we still maintain.

Suddenly, less than one year after the loss of my son, I inherited one hundred new sons and ten coaches. These young men, most of them the age of Forest, practically saved my life. I listened to their problems, hugged them when they needed hugging, cried with them when we lost (which was too often!), and became surrogate father to many of them. Over the years I baptized some, married others, and have felt close to them all as they have grown into young men and fathers.

One thing I learned about football players: they may have bodies that weigh 250 pounds and stand six-feet-five-inches tall, but underneath they are still eighteen-year-old boys who need fathers, mothers, coaches who understand, and a chaplain willing to accept them as persons, not merely football players.

These young men and their coaches, along with the church, became my family. Prior to every game I conducted a worship service for them, often in the chapel at Fifth Avenue or on the road in some motel's dining area. At times they came as a team to the Sunday morning worship service and, as I termed it, tilted the church on the side they sat. They allowed me to reinvest my love. I was discovering God at the point of cure as those young men challenged my best insight and energy.

Years ago I heard a minister say, "People pray and pray for God to use them. Well, get usable," he said, "and God'll wear you out!" As I became more usable to God, opportunities to reinvest my love and life and energy were coming faster than I could handle. I was on the verge of wearing out. Parents who had lost children started seeking me out for counseling. My loss of Forest had given me credibility beyond my training. And I was learning that every time a child dies, I lose Forest all over again. And this is draining, especially during intense counseling sessions.

While reinvesting one's love and energy is imperative, there are times one must exercise restraint. For instance, one mother who had lost her son joined a support group for mothers who had lost children. She was intense in her participation in every meeting. She told me she had been in the group for five years but had made little progress in working through her own grief. When asked how she participated in the sessions, she told me that every month, for the benefit of the newcomers in the group, she recounted in detail her son's accident, her feelings at the time, and what she did each day for the first six months following his funeral.

As we talked, we both became aware that in her willingness and attempts to help others and reinvest her love, she was not allowing her own wound to heal. We came to the rather graphic conclusion that as her wound would begin healing, she would tear the scab off at each meeting, and the bleeding would begin again. Although she was a leader in the group, I suggested that she retire from her five-year stint and give her own hurt and wound time to heal. After explaining her situation to her peers, she did resign from the group. Within months, she later related, she was able to get beyond her pain and reinvest her love in more constructive ways.

In my own situation, I knew I could not emotionally handle every tragedy that came to my office for help. I needed more resources.

Over breakfast one morning at Cabell Huntington Hospital, where I was to speak to the graduates in lab technology, I had a conversation with Ray Champ, the hospital's president. In the course of our conversation, I observed that the greatest need in our community was for a counseling service where pastors could refer people for depth counseling, as well as receive additional training themselves.

To my delight Ray was vitally interested. He had previously worked at a hospital with a strong chaplains' program and was open to discussion about forming a similar program at Cabell Huntington.

We arranged for North Carolina Baptist Hospital's Mac McGee, an expert in pastoral care programming, to meet with the executive committee of the hospital's board of trustees. Within a year following Mac's presentation, a board-certified chaplain, David Carl, founded a pastoral care program at Cabell Huntington, complete with a Clinical Pastoral Education department that would train seminary students and local pastors alike.

With this community resource going full throttle, I was able to lessen my counseling load with parents who had lost children and, at the same time, could refer them to expert counseling at a most crucial time in their lives. Discovering God at the point of cure was happening in my life, and soon in ways I never dreamed possible.

Not too long after going to Fifth Avenue, Faye and I were visiting my parents at the old home place during an August heat wave. A nurse who lived nearby, and a close friend of our family's, came by to check Mom's and Dad's blood pressure. "Why don't you check mine?" I asked, bragging that I had always had textbook blood pressure, 110 over 80.

On her first try she looked intently at the meter, frowned, and said, "I did something wrong. Let me do that again." After three times she finally said, "Your blood pressure is not textbook. It is 165 over 110!"

When we arrived back in Huntington, I went immediately to our family physician, who found my blood pressure had returned to its usual reading. While there I asked that his nurse irrigate my left ear to clear the wax, a procedure she had done many times for me. But this time water became trapped in my ear, and I was referred to a specialist, Dr. Kenneth Wolfe. In moments he had cleared up the problem. As I was about to leave, he asked, "How long have you had that knot behind your left ear?"

"Ten years at least," I said.

"Well, I don't like the looks of it," he said. "When you return to town I want to have a look at it. I'll measure it now and we'll see if it grows any in the next two weeks."

When I finally made the promised appointment with Dr. Wolfe, the calendar was showing the middle of September. He measured the growth and indicated that it had grown too much in the past few weeks. "We've got to get it out," he said, and the tone of his voice suggested his seriousness. "I want to have that thing in my hand," he said. "Now, when can we do it?"

I looked at Faye, she looked at me, and I said, "Our Becky is getting married November 7. We can do the surgery after that."

"No way," the doctor said. "I want to do it immediately if not sooner. How about October 1?"

"That's only one month before the wedding," I protested.

"You'll be okay by the wedding. I'm not worried about the

wedding, but I am worried about you. Go home and think about it and call me first thing in the morning to let me know."

After prolonged discussion, Faye and I (mostly Faye) decided we should follow the doctor's advice and have the surgery before the wedding. Arrangements were made. We went by Dr. Wolfe's office two days before the surgery for a final briefing. At that time he revealed the seriousness of the situation and all the things that could go wrong.

"You may have a speech impediment," he said. "Your speech could be slurred, and there may be a hole in the side of your face about the size of a lemon." He may have outlined more possible negatives, but when he told me my speech might be slurred I didn't hear much else. *God,* I said, half-prayer, half-oath, *what does a preacher do with slurred speech?*

The surgery took eight and a half hours as Dr. Wolfe extracted the tumor which had enveloped my parotid gland like an ivy vine wrapping itself around a large oak tree. The doctor had to trace each vine down every limb and twig, carefully cutting it out without damaging the seventh nerve, which controls the left side of the face. One slip of the knife and he'd have a preacher with slurred speech.

There are some two dozen physicians in Fifth Avenue Baptist Church, and Dr. Wolfe said it seemed every one of them came by several times during the surgery. One physician went home for dinner and told his wife, "You'll never hear our pastor preach again. No one can handle the seventh nerve for that long without doing permanent damage."

When I awakened in the recovery room doctors were all around me. I chanced opening one eye to see what was going on. "He's coming around," one of them said. And with that, Dr. Wolfe leaned over me and said, "Little buddy, can you smile?"

Of course, they had no way of knowing if the operation was a success until I was awake and able to respond to their verbal examinations. I didn't answer immediately. I was trying to sense feeling in my face. Again, leaning closer, Ken Wolfe asked, "Can you smile? Will you try to smile?"

I knew I could. "Smile?" I asked. "Smile? Man, I can whistle." And did.

Later that evening in my room, Dr. Wolfe came by for a visit. I was alert, hungry, and ready to talk. "Ken," I said. "Thanks. Thanks for everything."

"Don't thank me," he said in honest humility. "The first five hours were mine. The next three and a half you were in the hands of the Great Physician. There's no way you and I could have gone through that surgery without God's help." I know many physicians and persons of science hesitate to use the word *miracle,* but many of them who knew the inside story of my surgery used the M-word without fear of scientific ostracizing.

During the days of recovery I reflected upon the *cure* I had experienced. I wondered (and still do) why I was granted a miracle and Forest was not.

In my first sermon back at Fifth Avenue I said, "When Forest died I asked, 'Why him?' After my rather serious bout with surgery that could have rendered me silent as a preacher, I asked, 'Why me?' I'll never know the answer to my first question, but by the grace of God I will search diligently to learn the answer to my second question," I promised.

I have never reconciled why one person lives and another dies; why one is graced by a miracle and another is denied. But I have discovered that God's participation is always found at the point of cure, and that cure takes various forms. What God had in mind for me when he granted that miracle, I don't know. But for the past sixteen years, I have tried to find out. Maybe the search for meaning is the meaning; perhaps in the seeking lies the goal we seek.

I think Paul was right: "Keeping the faith" is the essence of life that enables us to "finish the course," however rocky or ill drawn it may be. And it is strength "to finish" that God offers, not assurance of achievement.

Chapter Thirteen

As events moved me rapidly into the morning of duty, there was a piece of unfinished business from the night of grief to which I had to return.

My questions surrounding the Lazarus incident were somewhere on a nail in the closet of my mind where I had hung them for the past months. Though I had coped rather well with the loss of Forest in terms of my emotional rehabilitation, and though I was writing new chapters in my life and reinvesting my love, the underlined and tear-blurred thirty-seventh verse of John's eleventh chapter still haunted me: "Could not he who opened the eyes of the blind man have kept this man from dying?" I needed biblical insight and theological perspective on this rather practical question raised by friends of Mary and Martha as they gathered at Lazarus's tomb.

Over that passage in the margin of my study Bible I had written: "How about Forest, also?" While I had moved on with my life, I had not moved beyond that Scripture and my marginal notation. I had to get back to it. Somehow I had to resolve that question, or at least put it to rest.

Early one morning, as I had many times during the first months following Forest's death, I read and reread that Scripture. I had always stopped with verse 37 and my marginal question. But this time I decided to finish the passage.

In the next sentences, I read: "Then Jesus . . . came to the tomb . . . and said, 'Take away the stone'" (John 11:38, 39 RSV). Something started happening in my thinking. Stones that had blocked my vision for so long started rolling down my theological hillside. For the first time I saw something I had never seen before.

When Jesus came to the tomb that held their grief and devastation, he didn't bother to answer their question about why he didn't keep Lazarus from dying. And he didn't deal with the cause of Lazarus's death. He dealt with solutions, not answers. He started moving toward the cure, refusing to spend much if any energy on questions about cause.

As I sat there, almost stunned with the light beginning to filter through the door of a half-opened tomb, etched in two thousand years of Christian history, I started seeing *how* God comes to my cure. My faith—birthed in the cradle of a Christian home, nurtured by a loving family, defined in schools of divinity, refined in challenging pastorates—told me that whatever difficulty came down the pike, God would be there, not to eliminate the problem but to give strength to deal with it. This I believed.

But as I reread the passage, God's *how* revealed the process God may sometimes use to meet me at the point of cure, enabling me to meet whatever challenge I encounter, granting strength and patience to endure. God comes to my cure not by answering my questions, not by giving me reasons, not by serving me with philosophical jargon, but (after I have rolled away a few stones) God comes, as Jesus did, by walking to the door of my grief-tomb, my pain-tomb, my why-tomb, and calling *my* name: "Come out," he yells. "Come out." It was *my* name he was calling, not Lazarus's, not Forest's. For the first time since Forest's death I came to realize that Lazarus was not my dead son.

I was Lazarus.

I had become entombed by a tragedy that happened to one I loved more than life itself. My own tomb wrappings had locked me in a grave like that of Lazarus, cutting off circulation of life-sustaining power, isolating me from the fresh air of faith that promised I could live again. Not many people sensed my inner struggle with the bandages I had allowed to bind my soul. But down deep inside I was bound as tight as Lazarus.

And like Lazarus, I staggered out of that tomb, trailing the mud of my own self-pity, flinging bandages right and left, and rubbing darkness from my eyes. When Lazarus staggered out of the tomb, Jesus gave a strong and specific command: "Unbind him, and let him go" (John 11:44 RSV).

Sitting alone in my study some twenty-four months after Forest's death and staring at the two-thousand-year-old story of Lazarus coming out of the tomb, I realized that God had had some help in bringing me back to life, and bringing life back to me. Looking back over the journey I had made through the "valley of the shadow," I knew many people had helped unbind me. I came to know the truth of an old statement I picked up somewhere along the line. I cannot recall its source, but its insight was dynamic for me: *"You alone can do it, but you can't do it alone."* In big ways and small ways, sensitive persons had helped unwrap the mummy-like bandages that had imprisoned me and had nearly given me a life sentence.

In one of the hundreds of letters we received following Forest's death, a friend wrote, "I sense you are on the road to healing because I experienced gratitude in conversation with you." I had not thought of gratitude as a vehicle that moves one along on the road to healing. I did have gratitude for Forest, for my family, and certainly for the many people who touched my life in the wilderness. As I reflected upon our friend's statement, it started making sense. Perhaps gratitude not only brings healing but is the point where healing begins. When the mind and heart look back, finding things to be thankful for, gratitude surfaces and gently pours balm on troubled waters, and navigation becomes possible again.

I am grateful for every card, letter, phone call, and personal word of comfort and encouragement I received from those people who, true to Jesus' command, have had a part in unwrapping me.

Unwrapping persons to whom Christ has given life is the age-old task of the church, and never more needed than when loss has devastated a person almost beyond recognition. But friends and family can only "unbind" so much. There was a part of the unwrapping process that only I could do.

My participation in the unwrapping process was made possible by a foundation laid in the early years of growing up under the influence of my pastor-grandfather. When I'd drop by his study after school for a brief visit, he would always ask, "Well, my son, what did you learn today?" Papa Benfield's question was not intended to intimidate but to stimulate. And it did. I dared not enter his study unless I had some tidbit of new data to spin out for him. He always received seriously whatever new information I shared, no matter how simple or trivial. And he would commend me. I see now that his commendation was more for my seeking new information than for the value of the specific piece of information.

As I look back eighteen years over the journey I have traveled since the loss of Forest, I hear Papa Benfield's question again, as I heard it hundreds of times during my pilgrimage, "Well, my son, what have you learned from all of this?"

Frankly, I'm not sure what *learning* is. If learning means experience laced with questions that still haunt, yes, I've learned some things. If it means faith beyond knowledge of what is seen, yes, there are some faith insights I've gained on the trip. If learning means recognizing reality but not necessarily understanding it, yes, I've experienced much learning.

The best example of not understanding reality happens when I walk not three football fields from where I'm writing this book to the little cemetery of my ancestors and stand before two grave markers, both reading: *Robert Forest Smith*. One marks the final resting place of my father: age eighty-four. I understand that marker. The other tombstone is for my son: age seventeen. I'll never understand that one.

But somewhere in this mystery of what I cannot understand, but must accept, stands God. I have learned that what I have believed and preached about God is true: that God is loving, redemptive, forgiving. And God's strength and grace are sufficient in times of trouble. I've learned that God moves in mysterious ways and that his mysteries scare me half to death at times. I've learned that God can take anything I lay on him when I'm angry at him, his universe, and the laws that govern it.

And I've learned as never before the meaning of John 3:16: "For God so loved the world that he gave his only begotten son . . ." That verse of Scripture took on a new meaning for me when I stood over the body of my only son.

I've also learned that God allows no experience to be wasted if I give him half a chance with me. To look at a negative incident and toss it away is a waste of energy. It is "throwing out the baby with the bath water."

When Jacob wrestled all night with "a man" (angel?), he would not allow the experience to be wasted. He declared in no uncertain terms: "I will not let you go, unless you bless me" (Genesis 32:24-32 RSV). Jacob refused to allow the night of adversity to pass without gleaning from it something for the future: a blessing. So great was that adverse experience that Jacob named the scene of battle Peniel, which means "For I have seen God face to face, and yet my life is preserved."

That night Jacob was wounded in the battle and forever after walked with a limp. An interesting and instructive phrase follows Jacob's experience: "The sun rose upon him as he passed Penuel, limping" (Genesis 32:31 RSV).

The evening of death and the night of grief wounded me, there's no doubt. I have scars from the battle—big scars, emotional scars, perhaps physical and mental scars. I wrestled with the angels of theology, philosophy, and psychology, to mention only a few. My faith was tested to the core. But there came a day, not one I can mark on the calendar of chronos, but a time of kairos when I knew that out of this tragedy God would bring some sort of blessing for my future.

Like Jacob, I walked and still walk with a limp. I always will. And like Jacob, I believed the sun would rise for me I as made my way to Ezekiel's morning of duty. In both evening and night I made a commitment: I would not allow the tragedy of Forest's loss to become an even greater tragedy by losing my own way, both present and future, as I lived out the morning that would come.

I faced two choices in the tragedy and loss: Waste the experience or use the experience. In my saner moments I knew not even God could help me if I shut all doors to healing and the future. Writing about the children of Israel's forty-year sojourn in the wilderness, the author of Hebrews was clear: "So we see that they were unable to enter [the Promised Land] because of unbelief" (Hebrews 3:19 RSV).

The choice was obvious: unbelief in God's power to take me out of the wilderness would keep me, like the Hebrews, in the wilderness, or like Lazarus, in the tomb. In either analogy the bottom line is the same. I know that God *cannot* if I *will not*. As limitless as God's power is, I have the capability of limiting him by unbelief and unwillingness to learn from and through tragedy. I can waste the experience.

In the process of "using the experience," I reviewed the picture of death in a way not possible before the loss of Forest. I learned that death is a reality, but not a morbid reality unless I refused to deal with it. We're tempted to view the lives and legacies of departed loved ones as revered relics placed under the glass case of memory, never to be touched but to be regarded only in hushed silence. In doing so, we refuse memory's efforts to stimulate positive remembrances.

As I searched for Forest's legacy—the gift of his life—I came to see that the legacy left by lost loved ones is not placed around our necks as an albatross but as an inner tube of strength and buoyancy, lifting and setting us in paths of the great currents of history.

A true legacy, I came to feel, is not bestowed as a tradition or life plan to be carried out but as a strength and a blessing for use as resources in living our own lives, playing our own games, with the assurance that memory will give freedom to be and to do.

As I looked at Forest's short but full life, I sensed a rare legacy from him that was totally out of proportion to his life span. Such a legacy places us upon the shoulders of past persons, not at their feet to worship them, nor at their sides to walk in morbid fantasy, nor in front of them to tout their greatness, nor behind them to camouflage their weakness, but on their shoulders so that we can see better and farther and further and can grasp what God has for us to do in our day and generation.

Seeking to use Forest's legacy, and to implement the insights gained during the process of learning to live again, I knew my life could never be business as usual.

Occasionally when a fire has nearly destroyed a store or business office, a sign printed in large letters is placed over the ashes, declaring "Open—Business as Usual." You admire such courage, but you know the words are untrue.

Business as usual can never be again. Your life is being redefined, reevaluated, and there's no way you can pretend the tragedy didn't happen. You admit the hurt and cover certain bases, but you can never have business as usual. Nothing is ever the same again.

I've learned that there are some things in life that get broken beyond repair, but never beyond some use. It took me a long time to replace that period with a comma. "My life is broken beyond repair." Period. That's so tempting, so logical. It takes a lot of faith, hope, courage, and love to turn that period into a comma and add, "but never beyond some use."

I have come to believe that the tragedy of a tragedy is to allow it to settle and simmer, to refuse to discover anything in the dark but darkness. Darkness never gets anything but darker by itself. Yet just one flickering candle cannot be defeated by all the darkness of a hundred hells. Life does not get better by itself, but a flickering candle of faith pushes the darkness back and shows just enough landscape for the next step. And one step at a time is good traveling over rough terrain.

There are so many things about all this experience I cannot understand, even when I use every analogy and metaphor possible. The well-known Methodist preacher Ralph Sockman gives yet another analogy that makes sense for me: the structure of a ship.

There are parts of a ship that by themselves would sink. The engine would sink if placed in the water by itself. Thrown into the water, the propeller would sink. Almost everything needed to build a ship—steel, lumber, nails, bolts—would sink if thrown into the water separately. But when the parts of a ship are built together, they float.

"So with the events of my life," says Dr. Sockman. "Some have been tragic. Some happy. But when they all come together, they form a craft that floats. The craft of my life not only floats, but it is going somewhere. And in that I am comforted."[1]

Romans 8:28, a hallmark of my theology, accommodates a paraphrase based on my experience during the past eighteen years:

For I know that God works all the parts—all the events of my
    life—together
    so it floats.
And I know that God has somewhere for me to go,
    and something for me to do.

In the years since Forest died, I, along with my family, have
traveled many miles on sea and land, literally and figuratively. We
have felt pain as the boats of our lives rocked with storms whose
waves almost capsized us, drenching us with cold spray that blinded
us for the moment. On land we've felt pain as we rounded curves,
negotiated mountains and valleys, and were jarred by bumps and
potholes in the road.

But we've felt joy, too, as new roads opened to new experiences
with an ever-widening circle of friends who have become fellow
pilgrims on a journey called life. We know the joy of new ports-of-
call with soon-to-be friends standing on the dock, ready to embrace
us with love and support. Though there have been painful days to
endure, I would not trade any day of pain if I had to lose the memory
of joys as part of the deal.

Losing Forest has given me new appreciation for the old Greek
myth about a woman who came down to the River Styx to be ferried
across to the region of departed spirits. Charon, the kind ferryman,
reminded her that it was her privilege to drink of the waters of Lethe,
the legendary river whose water causes people to forget. "Drink of
it," he told her, "and you will forget the life you're leaving."

"I will forget how I suffered?" she eagerly asked.

"Yes, and you will forget how you rejoiced," Charon reminded
her.

"I will forget my failures?"

"And also your victories," the ferryman added.

"I will forget how I've been hated?" she asked.

"Yes, and how you've been loved," Charon said.

She paused to consider the whole matter. Then, the story goes,
she left the river Lethe, not tasting its erasing waters, preferring to
retain the memory even of sorrow and failure rather than give up
the memory of life's loves and joys.

In this journey of eighteen years, I have learned three realities:

First, to love deeply is to hurt deeply. Second, to live again is to reinvest one's love. Third, deep hurt can become a solid foundation for life lived deeply.

Only three weeks before Forest's fatal accident, he appeared in *Bright New Wings*, a musical presented by the youth of Hickory's First Baptist Church. He was the apostle John, one of the Sons of Thunder whose pastime was shooting butterflies with his six-shooter (the drama's effort to update the biblical story, casting John as a tough cowboy). But at the end of the drama, John's rebirth and commitment to Jesus Christ moved him to become a gentler person. In Forest's final scene as John, he becomes fascinated by the butterflies he had previously killed for sport. Speaking to the audience, he says:

> I know it sounds hard to believe; but I slowly held out
> > my finger,
> and you know what? That butterfly came and landed on
> > my finger.
> I hardly breathed as I gently lifted my hand higher, putting
> > the little creature level with my eyes.
>
> For a long moment we stared at each other.
> Finally, as I watched him flying off, I thought:
> How much alike we are—both free and alive
> after spending dark hours in a chrysalis.
>
> I had found my power.
> Jesus had freed me—in a wonderful and mysterious way.[2]

---

[1] Ralph W. Sockman, *The Higher Happiness* (New York: Abingdon Press, 1950), p. 47.

[2] *Bright New Wings,* music by Cynthia Clawson, words and lyrics by Ragan Courtney, arranged by Buryl Red (Nashville, Tenn.: Triune Music, 1977).

Epilogue

The old French proverb is as true as it is ancient: *To suffer passes; to have suffered never passes.*

The wounds of loss do heal, but their scars remain. And living with the scars becomes a creative challenge, especially during the early years following loss.

In our family's journey through the evening of death and the night of grief, on our way to the morning of duty, we discovered that establishing the Robert Forest Smith III Scholarship at Wake Forest University, Winston-Salem, North Carolina, was one of the most therapeutic means of dealing with our loss and with the scars we will always bear. At the time of Forest's death, our family provided an alternate opportunity to friends seeking ways to remember our son, suggesting gifts be made to the scholarship. Over $4,000 was given.

But the scholarship actually became a reality two months later, on Forest's eighteenth birthday, when the youth of Hickory's First Baptist Church, where I had served as pastor, held a Rock-a-Thon. The young people solicited from friends and businesses dollars for each hour they would rock in a rocking chair throughout the night. Young people from Hickory High School, as well as from around the state, gathered in the church's fellowship hall. When the night of rocking ended, over $16,000 had been raised by the youth, and the scholarship's principal then totaled over $20,000, enabling the granting of a thousand-dollar scholarship for the academic year of 1979-80. At least one scholarship has been granted each year, and more than twenty young people have attended Wake Forest with the help of the scholarship.

Each year when the admissions committee of Wake Forest

contacts us with the résumé of the student they feel best meets the criteria of the scholarship's purpose, the young man we loved so deeply is vividly remembered.

At this writing, the scholarship's principal is over $140,000.

We are currently in the process of transferring the scholarship from the College of Wake Forest University to its Divinity School, scheduled to open in 1998. We strongly support the action of the university's trustees in establishing the new school and have worked for its founding in a limited capacity since its inception some years ago.

Our family feels that the best use of the scholarship at the present time is to encourage young men and women to seek and receive the creative development that the school will offer, sorely needed in this new day and generation of ministry.

Although this book largely reflects my journey and perspective, each member of our family could write her own and, I hope, will do so in the years ahead.

Becky was graduated from the University of North Carolina, Chapel Hill, in 1980, as a Morehead Scholar. In 1981, she married Joe Galli Jr., and in time made us the proud grandparents of Brittany Leigh, Matthew Forest, Madison Rae, and Joseph Peter. They live in Phoenix, Maryland, just outside Baltimore.

Rachel's journey following the loss of Forest was difficult. After graduation from Hickory High School in 1980, she had difficulty deciding whether to go to college or get a job. "Actually," as she would phrase it, given her humorous bent, "I did both!"

She spent two weeks in her first college experience. The place and time were not right for her. Then she got a job but felt the need to attend college. After several jobs and as many colleges, she came to Huntington, lived at home, and attended Marshall University in our city. After two years she finally started to "get it together" and graduated with honors. Five years were needed for Rachel to process Forest's death and her grief.

In 1991 she married Marty Clay. They are the proud parents of Adam Forest and Ashley Catherine, and live in Greensboro, North Carolina.

I find it interesting but not strange that both sisters bestowed upon their sons the name of their brother, whose memory continues to bless and whose death still hurts.

The impact of losing Forest was felt deeply by our family, especially Faye. But during the intervening eighteen years she has coped grandly, reinvesting her love and energy in church and grandchildren. Her diary covers reams of paper, a source I used often in writing this book. Perhaps someday she will write her own book, but in a real sense she is coauthor of this one. She stayed with me throughout the entire experience of writing. When each part of the manuscript was completed, I would go downstairs, get a cup of coffee, and sit in the den as she read and reread the material, offering suggestions, making corrections, often challenging particulars. And she cried as she relived the days catalogued.

Our lives are different since the loss of Forest, but the difference has drawn us closer together. Like all couples, we have our spats, occasions that move us toward each other by momentarily separating us.

While we are near the magical age of retirement, such plans are not in our minds as we gear for a multimillion-dollar building program at Fifth Avenue Baptist Church.

We have special reminders of our days with Forest and of the eighteen-year journey we've made since his death. The youth drama described in the last chapter is a most vivid memory of him. The title, *Bright New Wings,* symbolizes our perception of him, especially in his role as John, whose identification with butterflies signals new life.

Butterflies remind us of Forest, and of new life for him and us. On special occasions in our lives, a butterfly suddenly appears, its presence loaded with symbolism for us.

On my first Saturday on the sideline as chaplain of the Marshall University football team, a beautiful butterfly came and perched on my shoulder and stayed there until a young player came to talk with me. The butterfly left, as if to say, "Now, give your energy and love to him."

The list of butterfly encounters over the years is long. As I finished the first draft of this book, a large butterfly passed twice by my upstairs window as if to signal something. I'm not sure what.

Several days later, as I finished editing the final draft, Faye and I were sitting on our deck under a large umbrella that shaded us as we sipped coffee. The umbrella was only half-raised, but a beautiful butterfly came, worked its way inside the low-swinging canvas, almost on top of us, and then settled in for a spell. After some minutes it left, waving its wings as if to say, "Thanks for the memories."

I don't need butterflies to remind me of resurrection and new life, but they do remind me of that day when Forest, in the drama, said of the butterfly: "How much alike we are—both free and alive / after spending dark hours in a chrysalis." He then added, "I had found my power. / Jesus had freed me—in a wonderful and mysterious way."

And to both declarations I can say, "Amen," and "Me, too!"

A Letter to My Son

My Dear Son,

The hundreds of friends and scores of relatives who flooded our home for the past few days have returned to their daily run of duty. I sit alone in your room, the place where you and I have spent many, many hours, talking, discussing, raising more questions than we ever found answers for.

All the scaffolding of your short seventeen years stands in deafening silence—the catcher's mitt, bulletin board laden with girls' pictures, homecoming ribbons, stubs of special college football tickets, and a few mementos you never told me just what significance they held locked in their mute grasp.

Your drums that often rocked the house (and neighborhood) stand silent, never again to feel the rhythm of your body and soul. Wrinkled basketball shoes, a student council T-shirt with "President" stenciled on the back, a calendar stuffed with never-to-be-completed activities, rough drafts of term papers, an unfinished college application blank, and assorted books lie much as you left them on your desk.

A well-worn and daily-read Bible lies beside your bed, in easy reach. And a German shepherd named Deacon roams frustratedly in and out of your room, often pausing to lie on the foot of your bed, wondering why you and I have not had any late-night conversations there recently.

Son, you were doing something you loved—water skiing—

when it happened. Of course by now you know the whole story and understand more about everything than we ever will. We still wonder in the wordless silence of questioning spirits, trying to make sense of it all.

You touched so many lives in your short lifetime, more than most of us will ever touch in three-score and ten. In your life you touched hundreds; in your death you are touching thousands.

Yes, we are still asking WHY. Why did this happen? Why did it happen to you? Perhaps we'll never know the answer. Your mother, your sisters—Becky and Rachel—and I continue to ask this question with tears running unashamedly down our faces.

We are seeing many people's lives being changed through all this. And we are grateful. But in all honesty, our one desire is to have you back as you were—full of life, loving everybody you ever met, giving encouragement to people, dreaming dreams, making things happen, wrestling with me, getting ready for a date, washing the car, filling the rec room downstairs with guys under the pretense of studying chemistry (never knew chemistry to be that laugh-producing) and stuffing yourselves with so-called snacks that were in fact major meals! (Mom loved that.) We miss all that, and you, Son.

You and I discussed many questions during these past few years. Now you can find answers to them all. You beat me to it. I hope the first person you look up (after you experience the glory of standing face to face with God) is the apostle Paul. He left a lot of questions dangling. You remember some of them, don't you? Ask him to clear them up.

Then go find Simon Peter, that lovable, impulsive fellow who tried everything, accomplished some things, but in his attempts endeared himself to all who have ever slipped and fallen in their faith. You won't have much trouble recognizing him—you've lived in the same house with a guy like him for the past seventeen years!

Forest, we miss you. Our lives will never be the same again. We've learned a lot during these weeks about ourselves. And we've grown, matured.

I want to thank you for being the greatest son a father could ask for. I've never had to apologize for you or explain you. We have never worried or been concerned about you for a single moment.

Somehow you got it all together early, and you had your head on straight. People congratulate your mother and me on being good parents. But you know what? A good end in football makes the quarterback look great. Thanks for being a good end and making us look good.

You had just begun a course at school in Shakespeare. Soon you would have found a statement in *Julius Caesar* that your Dad feels describes you:

His life was gentle, and the elements
So mix'd in him that Nature might
    stand up
And say to all the world,
    "This was a man!"

And your family? We are struggling, my son, struggling. Our faith has been tested to the core. The rafters of our theology have trembled. We have touched the bottom, but I'm happy to report to you that the bottom is solid! We shall make it.

God keep you and God keep us all. We hurt, but we know that to hurt deeply is to have loved deeply.

Loving deeply,
    Dad

APPENDIX 2

Robert Forest Smith III's Essay for the Admissions Committee of Wake Forest University

The following essay was written by Robert Forest Smith III (1960–1978) only a few hours before his accident. It was to accompany his application to Wake Forest University. Applicants are required by the university to write about their goals, accomplishments, feelings, and, in general, about themselves. Forest would have restructured some sentences and edited severely, as was his custom. But we feel inclined to present it to you exactly as he had roughed it out in the creative hours of September 2, 1978.

Faye and R. F. Smith Jr.
October 1978

I feel one of my basic characteristics is that of being sensitive. This obviously has its advantages and disadvantages. Sometimes I'm too sensitive to what people say or think about me. I guess at times I'm too vulnerable. I've had to work with this situation a great deal because of my interest in leadership. The advantage of my sensitivity is that I can easily understand what offends others and avoid it. Sometimes it seems as though I can almost identify totally with others' feelings. This helps in developing and maintaining deep and meaningful relationships.

Another basic characteristic is perception. Sometimes I perceive things that hurt me deeply. Other times it helps me in understanding people and their feelings. It helps me to be more sensitive to their needs and wants.

Compassion plays an important role in my personality. It is easy for me to develop a special love for a person. I understand it is important to be open enough to people to accept them as who and what they are. I find it most interesting to initiate what seems to be a superficial relationship and develop it into a deep relationship. I guess I just have a special love for all people because of their individualities.

Another characteristic is pride. I'm pleased with who and what I am, but I'm never completely satisfied. I feel this is important. Pride and self-confidence have helped me through many elections, speeches and decisions. I feel you must believe in yourself before you can expect others to believe in you. To be perfectly honest, I'm proud of who and what I am, as well as what I've accomplished. I'm also proud of what I plan to accomplish in life. This helps to establish many goals in my life.

The fact or subject which I'm about to share is the most important. The subject is God. The fact is that I believe totally in him and Jesus Christ. I take very seriously my commitment to God. I also take seriously finding his purpose for my life. Now I feel as if the field of law and politics is my direction or area in life. I believe in daily prayer and reading of scripture. Both mean everything to me.

I believe my "religion" is personal. I'm not one to radically express my "fine lined" beliefs and preach damnation and hell fire to those who do not believe exactly as I. I respect the beliefs of others and I expect that respect in return. I try to make my beliefs as positive as possible, leaving out the "no no's" Christianity is so often burdened with. It bothers me for people to be so concerned about what "rules" others are breaking that they themselves are missing the major purpose and being of Christianity. However, that is their belief and I, although not agreeing, must respect them.

At times I can be very open about my faith, but those times must be with special sincere people in whom I trust. The last thing I want is to "turn off" others by boasting how great my religion and I are. This is a sensitive area because I've often been "turned off" by those who preach constantly of hell fire, damnation and "don't do this."

I want to try to reach those who have other needs similar to mine and expose them to the Lord. Again, my religion is very personal, but I love to share when possible.

I have several major interests, one of which is government. At present, I'm basing that interest locally in Student Government. This includes city-wide, divisional, District, and State and Regional Student Government. On each level I'm involved in some way in the governing body. I developed this interest several years ago while serving as a Governor's Page and helping in Broyhill's campaign. I maintained this interest by getting involved in Student Council. The more involved I get in Student Government, the more interested I become. I guess it's because I feel if I'm involved, I can help in doing what's best for the students. It gives me a feeling of service to more students than I could possibly reach any other way. (I believe I can help a greater number of people through government.) I believe my interest and love for Student Government can be easily transferred to the governments within the United States.

I'm interested greatly in learning as much as possible about Christianity. I like to read uncommon scripture in which there is much new thought. I also like to investigate special incidents in Jesus Christ's life. I find my religion and Bible a major interest, not only spiritually, but because of its mystery or my own lack of understanding.

Music is another interest which I like to be up-to-date on. It's difficult because of my other commitments, but I like to be exposed to all types of music. I've played the drums since the age of three and plan to continue.

Another interest is sports. This includes basketball, baseball, swimming, water skiing as a participant. All other sports I love as a spectator. It's very important to me to keep active and have fun, and sports is one great way.

My future plans (dreams) are easily explained, but will require long years of hard work. I hope to attend Wake Forest University and go into their law school. After graduating, I plan to set up a law practice (possibly going in with a group of successful lawyers). At the same time, I would like to get involved in local politics. As I develop as a lawyer, I hope to move up to the state level in government. My ultimate goal or dream is to be in the Senate. That's my dream on paper!

I've found several books that seem to "stay with me." One is *Death Be Not Proud*. It's a true story of a teenager who has a fatal tumor and keeps striving to give 100% to life. The book helped me to develop a new positive attitude toward not only life, but living it 100%. The courage shown by the boy still gives me a strength to keep striving for personal goals, no matter what the odds.

Native Son is a book which has taught me many things about emotions. Bigger is a black in the 1940's, who experiences many emotions and feelings and reacts in many different ways. I learned a little about the impact of peoples' reactions and responses on others.

The Grapes of Wrath was a reinforcement of the belief or theory (fact) that tragedy develops unity. A family composed of many different personalities is exposed to a number of negative elements in a journey west. The book exemplifies reactions and responses of basic personalities and the effect they have on each other. It also exemplifies the sacrifices that result in the unity caused by tragedy.

I found most astounding of all the simplicity of *The Old Man and the Sea* by Ernest Hemingway. I enjoy the simple story itself, but even more I enjoyed the symbolism. I've written several papers on Hemingway alluding to Christ and the crucifixion. Part of my interest came from research in the Bible and Biblical devices. When finding possibly "new" allusions, it was the feeling of discovery that developed in me a love for the book, as well as a love for the writing style of Hemingway. It intrigues me to read such simplicity and interpret it into many deeper meanings. There have been so many deeper meanings associated with Hemingway's *The Old Man and the Sea*, that maybe he himself might have to pause and think of these possibilities.

I've learned to be open to all literary works and realize each has something new or different to teach.

I can't give a total picture of myself without mentioning my relationship with my family. My family is one of the most important things in my life. We've all developed an open and honest relationship over the years. I experience the majority of my mental and spiritual support from my family. We've all felt much happiness and satisfaction through each other's love and accomplishments. Respect plays a large part in our family. We respect each other's ideas, beliefs and dreams. This lets us feel totally free to share with the other members in the family. This prevents many problems from occurring, as well as solving many more quickly. I'm very proud of the relationship of our family. I would change nothing.

R. Forest Smith III
September 2, 1978